JERZY KOSINSKI:
LITERARY ALARMCLOCK

JERZY KOSINSKI: LITERARY ALARMCLOCK

By *Byron L. Sherwin*

Cabala Press
Chicago, Illinois

Printed in the United States of America
ISBN 0-941542-00-9
© *copyright, Byron L. Sherwin, 1981*
copies available from Cabala Press
6424 N. Sacramento, Chicago, IL 60645

For my father,
who taught me how
to question answers

ACKNOWLEDGEMENTS

The support of family and friends helps temper the otherwise lonely task of research and writing. While working on this book, the aid of a number of individuals proved invaluable.

To Jerzy Kosinski who freely gave of his time and of his advice, both in personal interviews and in telephone conversations, I am singularly grateful. In articulating a portrait of his vision, the acuity of my own self-reflective vision has become immeasurably enhanced.

To Katherine von Fraunhofer for providing me with written material by and about Kosinski which otherwise would have escaped my notice, and for her kindness, I owe a debt of gratitude.

To Rosemary Krensky and Rosaline Cohn I am indebted for their friendship and for their support of my work.

To Dr. Sheldon Berger, I am grateful both for his care and for his caring.

To Arnost Lustig, Lowell Komie, Beverly Yusim, Susan Ament and Janet Stern who read early drafts of this manuscript and contributed helpful and insightful suggestions, I offer a "thank you."

To JoAn Goldin, whose friendship is one of the most treasured gifts granted me, I am thankful for the many hours of discussion regarding the contents of this work during the months of its composition. Her design of this volume's cover expresses on a single sheet of paper that which it has taken me many sheets of paper to articulate.

To my wife Judith, who must share the frustrations and the doldrums I inevitably encounter when I am writing, my most sincere appreciation for her continued understanding and for her perseverence. The gift of her love makes possible much of the impossible.

To my parents, and especially to my father to whom this book is dedicated, I offer gratefulness for their sustained concern for me, and for their continued interest in my work. My virtues derive from their guidance. My deficiencies derive from myself.

Chicago, Illinois
October 29, 1981

Table of Contents

Fairy Tales and Nightmares

What kind of bizarre fairy tale would have emerged had Hansel and Gretel been young Jews or Gypsies wandering alone in eastern Europe during the Second World War? Would they have been able to escape the clutches of a dragon whose fiery breath consumed over a million children? Would they have managed to push the evil witch into an oven, or, would an oven have become their own final destination? Could the fertile imagination of Jonathan Swift have conjured up an image of a six-year-old child Gulliver wandering about lands of Nazi conquest, provinces populated by death camps?

From the ages of six to twelve Jerzy Kosinski wandered alone through war-torn eastern Europe. Unlike Little Red Riding Hood, no hunter appeared to save him from the wolves he encountered. Unlike children in fairy tales, he did not return home to live "happily ever after." Rather, he returned home to find himself a stranger. Restored to his place of origin, he discovered that his odyssey was only beginning.[1]

Jerzy Kosinski was born in Lodz, Poland, of Jewish parents, on June 14, 1933. His father was a classical philologist and his mother was a pianist. In 1939, soon after the Nazi invasion of Poland, Kosinski was separated from his parents and was cast adrift in rural Poland for the duration of the war. His childhood abruptly hijacked, Kosinski was unexpectedly transferred from kindergarten to an elementary school of survival. The curriculum of Kosinski's new "school" included brutalization, humiliation, starvation, exposure and ostracization. The major subjects were beatings, robbery, rape and attempted murder. At the age of nine, in a confrontation with a hostile peasant crowd, Kosinski lost the power of speech.[2]

Returning home in 1945, Kosinski discovered that few members of his large family had survived the Holocaust. Scores of familiar faces literally had vanished into smoke.[3] The innocent child he once had been had vanished as well. The naive boy who he had been had metamorphosed into an adolescent virtuoso in the art of survival.

With the "liberation" brought about by the end of the war, a period of spiritual confinement began. Back home in his native city with his parents, the young Kosinski felt like a butterfly freed from its cocoon only to find itself trapped in a glass cage. As a childhood Gulliver, Kosinski had pursued his precarious though unconfined existence in the hamlets and forests of rural Poland. However, upon his return home he found himself increasingly stifled by the life-style which characterized communist Poland in the post-war era. In Kosinski's view, the restrictive atmosphere of the state-controlled environment of post-war Poland traumatized him more severely than the experiences he endured during his six years of wandering. A resident alien in his native city, the young Kosinski was now a refugee without refuge.

Upon his return, Kosinski was placed in a school for the handicapped because of his mute condition. After two years in that school, he was transferred, still mute, to be taught to read and write by his father and by private tutors. At the age of fifteen he regained the power of speech – absent for six years – in a skiing accident. Completing high school in one year, he entered the University of Lodz.

The pariah status Kosinski had experienced as a boy continued during his teenage years. As a Jew, whose appearance distinguished him from other Poles, he was an object of discrimination and social exclusion. His refusal to espouse the official communist doctrine led to his suspension at the university on two occasions.

Despite these obstacles, Kosinski managed to obtain both a Master of Arts in History (1953), and a Master of Arts in Political Sociology (1955) from the University of Lodz. Subsequently, he became the youngest associate professor and state grantee at the Polish Academy of Sciences in Warsaw. During the winters he was employed as a skiing instructor in the Tatra Mountains and during the summers as a social counselor and horseback riding instructor at a resort on the Baltic Sea. Because of his knowledge of foreign languages, his academic status, his organizational skill, and his non-aligned political position, Kosinski was drafted by organizers of the 1955 Festival of Youth in Warsaw and the 1957 Youth Festival in Moscow to help run the foreign (i.e., mostly non-Communists) honorary guest departments at these two events. The Moscow festival provided Kosinski the opportunity to observe Soviet society up close.

In the 1950's Kosinski elected the study of photography and photographic chemistry as an academic minor. By 1957 he was a prize winning photographer whose photographs were exhibited at more international exhibitions than anyone else's in eastern Europe.

The Stalinization of Poland convinced Kosinski that there was no place for him in such a society. Despite his privileged position as an academician in Poland, Kosinski decided to escape to the West. The collectivist mentality of eastern European communism and his own philosophy of individualism were clearly irreconcilable. Kosinski's plan of escape would seem like a literary contrivance were one to read of it in a novel.

Vowing that he could not be kept in eastern Europe against his will, Kosinski risked a long prison sentence in order to secure his freedom. First, he created four fictitious members of the Academy of Sciences to act as his "sponsors." Using his access to government printing plants, he furnished each of these fictitious individuals with the appropriate official seals, stamps and stationery. Then, for two years Kosin-

3

ski maintained a correspondence between these individuals and government agencies. With the recommendations of three of his four "sponsors," Kosinski secured a forged "Chase Manhattan Fellowship" which enabled him to secure an exit visa from Poland. With a cyanide capsule under his tongue, lest he fail in his escape attempt, Kosinski left Poland for the United States. On December 20, 1957, he arrived in New York City.

No longer an "inner emigré trapped in spiritual exile", Kosinski was now a destitute immigrant with virtually no knowledge of English. Kosinski's father, a linguist, provided him with a correspondence course in the English language. Within six months, Kosinski added English to the list of almost a dozen languages he either speaks or reads.

To support himself after his arrival in the United States, Kosinski was employed in such diverse jobs as a truck driver, a parking lot attendant, a cinema projectionist, a paint scraper, a portrait photographer, and a chauffeur for a black nightclub entrepreneur. In 1958, a Ford Foundation fellowship allowed him to resume his doctoral studies in social psychology. For the next four years, Kosinski was enrolled at Columbia University, and at the New School for Social Research.

In Poland, in 1954 and 1955, Kosinski had published his masters' theses. In 1960, he made his English publishing debut. *The Future Is Ours, Comrade* a socio-political analysis of Russian life was published under the pen-name, Joseph Novak. Kosinski, who occasionally now wears a disguise to avoid recognition and to retain the privacy of anonymity, ironically chose to disguise the author of his first book which catapulted him out of anonymity. In this regard, Kosinski later remarked "a pen name allows you the fun of remaining anonymous and to openly recommend your books."[4] Such behavior is consistent with Kosinski's chosen motto, *Larvatus prodeo* – "I go forth disguised."

Serialized by *The Saturday Evening Post,* condensed in

Reader's Digest, and eventually translated into eighteen languages, *The Future is Ours, Comrade* became a bestseller. While writing a sequel, *No Third Path* (published in 1962 also under the name of Joseph Novak), Kosinski met (on a blind date) and continued to date Mary Hayward Weir, the young widow of the American steel magnate, Ernest T. Weir. Two years later, in January 1962, they were married.

Upon his marriage to Mary Weir, the child who not so long before had lived among the peasants of wartorn rural Poland, now found himself living in sumptuous luxury among the leaders of American industry and high society. The adolescent who grew to manhood in communist Poland was now living as an adult among those who composed the American corporate and political power structure. A life of nightmares had become a life of fairy tales. However, this chapter in Kosinski's life was to end precipitously with Mary Weir's death from cancer in 1968.

It was during his marriage to Mary Weir that Kosinski turned toward writing fiction. Kosinski's first novel, *The Painted Bird,* is about a homeless boy in eastern Europe during World War II, and it reflects an existence he had experienced as a child. Though presently translated into almost thirty languages, with sales in the millions, *The Painted Bird* was originally rejected by sixteen American publishers.

After Mary Weir's death, Kosinski taught for a number of years at Wesleyan University, Princeton University and Yale University. In 1968, his second novel, *Steps,* was published. This work, written with the assistance of a grant from the Guggenheim Foundation, was awarded the National Book Award in 1969. A succession of subsequent novels followed: *Being There* 1971, *The Devil Tree* (1973) *Cockpit* (1975), *Blind Date* (1977), *Passion Play* (1979), and *Pinball* (1982). At present, more than sixteen million copies of Kosinski's work have been sold throughout the world.[5]

Kosinski continually rewrites and reworks his novels. Second editions of his books often incorporate changes from the first published edition. For example, the original 1965 edition of *The Painted Bird*, differs substantially from the "complete edition," published in 1970. The paperback edition of *Passion Play* incorporates minor alterations not found in the original hardcover edition. *The Devil Tree* (1973) now appears in a revised and expanded edition (1981).[6] Because Kosinski regards his books as his "only spiritual accomplishment," he writes (in the words of one critic) "as if each word costs $1000."[7] Spending approximately three years on a novel, Kosinski continually contracts the text, even after it has been set in galley proofs. For example, *Passion Play* was reduced in size by one-third after it had been set in type.

In addition to his novels, Kosinski authored a screenplay based on his novel, *Being There*. The 1980 film of that name starred Peter Sellers, Shirley MacLaine, Melvin Douglas and Jack Warden. Kosinski's screenplay won the best screenplay of the year award from both the Writer's Guild of America and the British Academy of Film and Television Arts. In 1981, Kosinski made his debut as an actor, playing the communist leader Grigori Zinovyev in *Reds,* a film directed by his friend Warren Beatty. A frequent guest on television talk shows, Kosinski also writes essays and articles for a wide variety of journals and magazines.

As president of the American center of P.E.N., Kosinski has been an activist in the struggle for human rights around the world. He has intervened on behalf of persecuted writers in many countries, and personally has financed the emigration of at least eighty friends and colleagues from totalitarian countries.[8] In addition, Kosinski has been active in the American Civil Liberties Union and in the International League for Human Rights. It is not unusual for Kosinski to visit hospital wards for the incurably ill in order to talk or to read to patients who feel abandoned.[9] In 1968, he met Katherina von Fraunhofer. Since then, she has been his constant companion, and a number of his works have been dedicated to her.

Jerzy Kosinski has lived many lives and has survived many encounters with death. His spirit already has undergone many transmigrations in the course of a life pregnant with adventure and marred with catastrophe. Kosinski's description of one of the characters in his books may be ascribed to him: Jerzy Kosinski is "his own event."[10]

Despite a life replete with surprises and contradictions where each subsequent moment represents a "blind date" with the future, Kosinski remains disciplined, organized and focused when it comes to his writing. Only then does he feel unified; only then do the contradictions and paradoxes which characterize his life make sense. In his words, "Fiction brings order into my life; it helps me define my environment."[11] In order to grasp the vision embodied within Kosinski's writings, it is first necessary to examine his views regarding the nature and function of art, his perspective on the nature and social function of literature.[12]

The Nature of Art

Events in the life of Jerzy Kosinski resemble events in the works Jerzy Kosinski. Events in the lives of the characters which populate Kosinski's novels parallel events in his own life. For example, like the nameless boy in *The Painted Bird*, Kosinski wandered as a child through rural Poland during the Second World War. Like the boy in that book, Kosinski was a mute for a number of years. In *Cockpit*, Kosinski's protagonist, Tarden, escapes from eastern Europe in a manner which approximates Kosinski's own mode of escape from Poland.[13] Levanter, the protagonist of *Blind Date*, has discussions with the Nobel Prize winning scientist, Jacques Monod. Monod had been a friend of Kosinski's.[14]

In *Blind Date*, Levanter is travelling from Paris via New York to the home of his childhood friend in Los Angeles. His luggage is mistakenly unloaded in New York. Levanter goes for the night to his New York apartment, planning to continue on to Los Angeles the next day. That night a gang breaks into the home of his friend killing those present. An unidentified man murdered there is thought to be Levanter. By chance, Levanter had survived the masacre.[15] Similarly, Kosinski had been en route to the home of his childhood friend, Roman Polanski, when his luggage was mistakenly unloaded in New York. Kosinski went to his New York apartment, assuming that he would continue his journey the following day. That evening the Manson gang invaded Polanski's home killing his wife, Sharon Tate, and five guests who were there. Since Kosinski was expected to have been there, an unidentified male murder victim was thought to be Kosinski.

Reflections of Kosinski's marriage to Mary Weir appear in his works. For example, Mary Weir died of cancer as did the wife of Lavanter, the protagonist of *Blind Date,* and Fabian, the protagonist of *Passion Play.*[16]

These are but a few examples of the close parallels between events in Kosinski's life and those in his works. Such parallels have led some interpreters of Kosinski's writings to claim that his novels, especially *The Painted Bird,* are more accurately designated autobiographical memoirs than fictional narratives.

Despite the similarity between events in his life and those in his works, Kosinski strenuously has maintained that his novels are works of fiction and are not autobiographical memoirs.[17] For critics of Kosinski's writings to consider his novels as autobiographical – even in part – ignores Kosinski's stated views regarding nature of art, the nature of literature, and the relationship between experience and art, between experience and literature.

Events and experiences in an artist's life may provide raw material for artistic expression. Were these events to remain purely subjective, however, they would be too intensely personal either for the artist to create or for his audience to grasp. Artistic expression therefore requires a distance, an "alienation," of the artist from the experience he might choose to reflect in his work. In Kosinski's words, "the artist's alienation from the specific experience seems to be an indispensable prerequisite for the creative process."[18] Paradoxically, artistic expression requires the objectivization of the subjective.

Once an experienced event occurs, it populates the province of past. As such, it is only accessible through the memory. Remembered events, in Kosinski's view, are fictions. The remembered event or experience is not the event or experience which has occurred; neither is it a duplication of the event or of the experience which has taken place. For Kosinski "the memory is our supreme writer and editor. It is the aesthetic dimension of our life."[19] The "fraudulent bookkeeper" — the memory — edits and shapes the experiences of past into scenarios of its own.[20] The memory remolds the past into little films. It reworks the past by creating many short-stories out of our experience. In Kosinski's words, "we fit experiences into molds which simplify, shape and give them an acceptable emotional clarity. The remembered event becomes a fiction, a structure made to accomodate certain feelings . . . There is no art which is reality; rather, art is the using of symbols by which otherwise unstateable subjective reality is made manifest . . . the actively creative mind edits out what is unimportant or non-communicable and directs itself toward fictive situations."[21] In this view, art is neither an actual event nor is it a totally created event without a basis in experience. It is a fictive event.

Art may accomodate "autobiographical elements," but it does not provide an "instant replay" of autobiographical experiences. For Kosinski, art is an event in itself. The fictional narrative is not totally detached from experience nor is it a product of *creatio ex nihilo*. The fictional narrative *"is an event as fiction."*[22]

The fictive event embodies a vision which provides a means whereby the individual may transcend the limitations of his experience and of his particular condition. For Kosinski, it is this ability of the human being to transcend his own self and his own condition which makes art possible. It is this possibility of self-transcendence which is the uniquely human characteristic.

The catalyst for self-transcendence is the imagination. A product of the exercise of the imagination is art. The confluence of imagination and memory creates a vision, a fictive event, by means of which the individual may transcend his own self and his condition. To deny the imagination is to reject that which makes us uniquely human, that which makes art possible.

To surrender the imaginative ability is to forfeit the possibility of modifying one's own existence, to yield one's prerogative of becoming a protagonist in the creation of one's own self. To cede the imagination is to render to others – family, society, the state – the option of imposing their vision upon our lives, their plot upon our existence, their destiny upon our experience. To permit others to edit the experiences of our lives, to create us in their image – from their imagination – is to authorize the indoctrination of our own imaginations. To surrender our individual vision is to commission others to compose the novel which is our lives.[23] Applying his aesthetic position to his political stance, Kosinski reminds us that the essence of totalitarianism is the attempt of the state to inflict its vision, its plot, upon the lives of its citizens.[24]

Kosinski's works are products of his vision, his memory, his imagination. As such, they are works of fiction and not autobiographical memoirs. However, their being fiction does not preclude them from being accurate and true. Perhaps because they are fiction, they are true. Like Nietzsche, Kosinski seems to affirm that truths *are* fictions. Like Nietzsche, Kosinski maintains that our vision of the world, our perspective of truth, are expressions of interpretive fiction. Hence, our truths are fictions, and our fictions are our truths. These truths, these fictions, are not a goal, but a bridge.[25] By means of these fictions, by means of imaginative vision, the human being may transcend himself; he may become more than he is.

The Function of Art

Many of the themes Kosinski explores in his writings are reminiscent of themes treated in the novels of the French existentialists.[26] However, next to the stark, chilling narratives of Kosinski's novels, the works of the French existentialists take on the bland flavor of detached treatises, of literary fabrications designed to deal with a philosophically contrived human condition. Compared to the boy of Kosinski's *Painted Bird*, the *angst* Camus' Meursault, and the "nausea" of Sartre's Requentin almost seem satirical comedies. Next to the horror inflicted upon Kosinski's vagabond boy, the dilemmas of Camus' "Stranger" and the anxieties of Joseph K. in Kafka's *The Trial* seem like pastoral tales.

Because of the naked horror of his narratives, Kosinski has been accused of "sick fantasizing," of writing perverted pornography, of brutalizing his readers, and of overstating the events he describes. In the words of one reviewer, "Kosinski's novels enjoy their popularity because of the public's prurient desire for continual arousal."[27] A second reviewer, writing about Kosinski's novel, *Cockpit*, remarks, "I cannot see what the retailing of such sick fantasizing can do but minister to wholesale sickness . . ."[28]

Such evaluations of Kosinski's writings may reveal more about the critics who formulate them than they do about the author and the works they purport to judge. It may be that such critics are merely revealing their own inability to accept the plausibility and the accuracy of Kosinski's vision of society and life, rather than offering a considered critique of the quality of his literary works. For example, those critics who perceive *The Painted Bird* as the product of a prurient and

12

sado-masochistic imagination, simply manifest an unschooled naiveté about the Holocaust event. Whereas critics unaware of the nature of the Holocaust describe *The Painted Bird* as too horrible to be plausible, Kosinski's friends in eastern Europe who had had experiences similar to his during the war find that work to be "a pastoral tale compared with the experiences so many of them and their relatives had endured during the war. They blamed me [Kosinski writes] for watering down historical truth . . ."[29]

No one familiar with the Holocaust would read Kosinski's work as a product of sheer imagination. After a confrontation with the Holocaust, one recognizes that the unbelieveable has become credible, that inconceivable events are now historical facts, that the horrors of the most ghastly of nightmares are now the constant memories of once innocent and once naive children. One of the characteristics which differentiates Holocaust literature from other kinds of literature is that in other genre of literature imagination transcends realism while in Holocaust literature, reality transcends the product of even the most procreant and the most ghoulish imagination.

The Painted Bird is set in Nazi-occupied eastern Europe during the Holocaust; nevertheless, it makes little direct reference to the process of destruction, to death camps, to gas chambers.[30] Kosinski prefers to convey the horror of the Holocaust by shocking us into feeling the terror of a single individual rather than by asking us to try abstractly to comprehend the pain, death and suffering of countless millions. The realistic power of Kosinski's narrative compels his reader to "feel" the traumas experienced by his characters. He refuses to permit his readers the luxury of reducing the events he describes to conceptualized symbols. He pulls his reader into becoming a participant in the fictive event.

Discussing a brutal scene of an eye gouging in *The Painted Bird*, Kosinski remarks:[31]

The concentration camp as such is a symbol you can live with very well. We do. It doesn't really perform any specific function. It's not as close to us as the eyesight is. When you describe the atrocity of the concentration camp you are immediately reminding the reader that this is not his reality. It happened, you say, it happened in such and such a place . . . But when you describe the eyes being gouged out, you don't make it easier for the reader, he cannot help feeling his own eyes disappearing. Somehow, becoming blind.

Kosinski is no nihilist. He forces us to confront horror. He coerces us to realize that each of us is a potential victim. For Kosinski, it seems, splinters of the Holocaust have survived World War II and continue to irritate and to infect the quality of our daily life. Kosinski forcefully reminds his readers that the trauma of victimization, amplified to a cacophonous degree during the Holocaust, continues in a modulated form in the post-Holocaust world. For Kosinski, failure to be aware of the trauma of victimization—past and present—nurtures a breeding ground for future victimization.[32] The stark, simple, jolting quality of Kosinski's narrative compels his readers to empathize with the victimized characters who populate his works. Like a nail scratched across a blackboard, Kosinski's words command his readers' acute attention. No one can remain untouched or unmoved. He prevents his readers from retreating into abstract complacency about the plight of the victimized, which potentially may be the fate of any of us.

Through his obsession with victims of brutality, Kosinski endeavors to goad his readers into recognition of the omnipresent remains of the Holocaust which continue to plague us, and to enjoin his readers to continue to combat those remnants.[33] For Kosinski, it appears, the Holocaust was like a cancer which damaged the body of human society. Though surgically removed with the defeat of Nazism, traces of the

Holocaust have nevertheless spread. Therefore, constant vigilance is required to control symptoms of this disease which can and do appear at any time and at any place. Kosinski attempts to awaken his readers to the fragile and precarious nature of daily existence. Throughout his writings, Kosinski explores the implications of human existence in a world in which the Holocaust is an omnipresent memory, and where universal incineration remains an ever present possiblity, where the fate of each individual, and perhaps of the world as a whole is "ashes to ashes."[34]

Neither the brutal scenes in *The Painted Bird,* nor those in Kosinski's other works can be dismissed as the literary contrivances of a warped mind. There is nothing in his fiction, Kosinski maintains, that cannot be substantiated by the daily national newspapers. There is nothing in his novels, Kosinski claims, that could not take place in any city block in any American metropolis. No scene in any of Kosinski's books is one from which either he or any of his readers can be assured of immunity.[35]

For Kosinski, the novelist is not a tourguide and the reader is not a voyeur on a tour of the scenery the novelist portrays. The aim of art is not to offer a copy of an event, but to be an event in itself. The goal of the novelist is to involve the reader in this event. If the reader bypasses the literary landscape and perceives the narrative as an abstract imaginative exposé of a distant realm and of distant people, then the artist has failed. What art is created to accomplish, what literature strives for, is the participation of the reader in the literary event, the assimilation of the literary event into the life of the reader. In Kosinski's words, "Fiction assaults the reader directly, as if to say: It is about you. You are actively creating this situation when you read about it; in a way you are staging it in your own life."[36]

In his work, through his work, Kosinski attempts to move the reader "from the waiting room into the examination room . . ." Once the reader is there, Kosinski observes, the reader is given a shock: "you are mortal, you're vulnerable, you're not protected, yet, you survive. It should be a joyful feeling, the awareness of being alive."[37]

Through his participation in the fictive event, the reader's own imagination may be provoked. By supplementing the text he reads with the products of his own imagination and with memories of his own experiences, the reader forges a bridge between the author and himself. By means of his imaginative confrontation with the author's quest for self-awareness, the reader is stimulated to deepen his own quest for self-awareness. Through his participation in the author's vision of the complexities and the nature of life, the reader is spurred on to edit and perhaps to revise his own vision of the nature of reality. In this view, art provides a means for a confrontation with and an awareness of the drama of existence, rather than offering an escape route from reality and from human existence. In this view, the reading of literature does not present a packaged tour to foreign realms. Rather, literature acts as a catalyst for confrontation with the conditions which epitomize daily existence.

For Kosinski, the purpose of art, like the purpose of life, is "to evoke a state of being aware as opposed to being merely mortgaged . . .", to tap the roots of consciousness in order to reawaken an awareness of life, to reject life as passive existence and to affirm life as a drama in which one is a protagonist and not an actor playing a role composed by others.[38] For Kosinski, the "social function of the writer is that of social detonator." The serious novelist's task is to take society to task.[39] The moral obligation of the author is honestly to share his vision with his reader. The goal of the artist is not so much creation as transformation.

Kosinski's novels articulate a vision of the precarious nature of human existence, of the omnipresent threat of victimization, of the fragil feature of human life, of the constant dangers which characterize life. Because his vision is grounded in experiences which are beyond the experiential parameters of most of his readers, Kosinski's work is often misinterpreted and misunderstood. In this sense he is like Fabian the protagonist of his novel, *Passion Play*. Fabian is an author who writes books about polo-playing. However, unlike other more popular authors, he emphasizes the dangers of the sport rather than its pleasures. His works are criticized for being excessively foreboding and brutal. The critics of his works fail to realize that they are intended as safety manuals for the inexperienced rider.[40] Kosinski's portrayal of polo may be a metaphor for life itself. Indeed, while teaching college, he offered a course called "Riding Through Life." Like Fabian, Kosinski has been criticized for emphasizing the bleak and the brutal by critics who fail to understand that his books may serve as safety-manuals aimed at increasing awareness of the dangers implicit in the game of life. Devoid of such an awareness, bereft of a safety-manual, the individual becomes a "painted bird," innocently vulnerable, oblivious to actual danger.

At a time when life has become a "spectator sport," the need for art to propel us into a confrontation with our own selves, with our own condition, with our own society, becomes an urgent *desideratum*. At a time when our social environment pressures us into becoming passive participants in our own existence, the function of art as a "social detonator" and the function of the artist as an "alarmclock" becomes increasingly necessary. According to Kosinski, "all art is a revenge against passivists; it combats deadening of the soul. The artist demonstrates that what he can see, we can see as well. A painter, a photographer, a filmmaker, a dramatist, an art critic, a novelist, a poet—each one of them is an awakener."[41] By means of the artist's vision, we may be awakened to an awareness of both the preciousness and the precariousness of our own existence. Through confrontation with the artistic vision of another, our own vision of reality may be evoked and our passion for life provoked.[42]

Looking For A Vision

Kosinski's literary vision already comes into focus in his first novel, *The Painted Bird*. The nameless boy protagonist of that work engages in a quest for a vision, for a source of morality, identity and meaning in a world characterized by horror and terror. At one point in the novel the boy seeks meaning and morality in religious faith.

Convinced that the world is governed by a just God who rewards those who demonstrate their faithfulness with penance and prayer, the boy believes that he now has found a focal point for meaning. Self-worth, personal meaning and inner fortitude would be guaranteed by a divine force which governs the affairs of the world. Believing that his suffering was not the product of human cruelty, but punishment for his own lack of piety, the boy becomes immersed in religious fanaticism.[43] He now maintains that only an alliance with God would insure power, justice and meaning:[44]

> I was ready to start a new life. I had all that was needed [i.e., prayers and faith] and gloried in the knowledge that the days of punishment and humiliation would soon be past. Until now I had been a small bug that anyone might squash. From now on the humble bug would become an unapproachable bull.

After being humiliated by his "master" and by the people in church who throw him into a manure pit, the boy is traumatized into becoming a mute. Convinced that a power other than God must be determining his destiny, the boy rejects religious faith. There was no reason, no justification for a just and benevolent God to "inflict such terrible punishment"

18

upon him.[45]

For Kosinski, God – if He exists – is an apathetic witness to human suffering. "Even the most overworked God could not overlook such a menace to his people."[46] Religion was a farce. Even the believers do not believe. For them God is "like the unexpected guest for whom the wealthier farmers always kept an additional place at their table."[47]

Toward the end of *The Painted Bird,* a Russian soldier named Gavrila saves the boy and becomes his protector. Gavrila convinces the boy that God does not exist, that "religion is a tale for ignorant people who do not understand the natural order of the world . . ." Religion is an invention of the clergy which they use to delude and to control the masses. Belief in God is only a refuge from individual responsibility, a crutch destined to collapse in time of need, a notion antithetical to the truth – that "people themselves [and not God] determined the course of their lives and were the only masters of their destinies."[48]

Having concluded that belief in God insures neither meaning nor justice, and convinced that to survive one must align oneself with the powers that control the world, the boy now seeks out a source of power other than the god who failed him.

Having already been identified by the peasants as a Gypsy or as a Jew who was assumed to be kin to the Devil and possessed by an evil spirit, the boy decides to forge an alliance with the demonic forces. The condition of this pact is that the more harm, evil, misery and pain one might inflict upon others, the more one could rely upon the demonic forces to aid one in the struggle for survival. But, the more one succumbed to emotions of benevolence, love, friendship and compassion, the more vulnerable to suffering, misery and extinction, one would become. The more diabolical one's actions, the greater one's ability to inflict evil would become. Goodness was characterized by weakness and passivity. Faith in God and justice had caused his muteness, his victimization, the boy reasoned. Now, by means of an alliance with evil, the boy believed, he would become like the Nazis, evil and invincible. No longer a passive powerless victim, he would now become a powerful protagonist.[49] As the war drew toward an end, and the "invincible" Nazis met defeat, the boy's faith in his pact with the demonic began to wane. From his Russian liberators, the boy was exposed to a new source of meaning, identity and morality – the communist state.

Like so many liberated from Nazism by the Russians, the boy is won over by the promises and the ideology of Communism.[50] The power which defeated the Germans, the army which brought liberation, the ideology which promised a world where all people are equal, where "there would be no rich and no poor; no exploiters and no exploited, no persecution of the dark by the fair, no people doomed to gas chambers", represented a source of meaning and security. Good does triumph over evil. Not the good taught by religion, but the good promised by those dedicated to the public good – the members of the Communist Party. It was the Party which insured improvement of the quality of life, the Party which defined each person's worth and each individual's importance.[51] No longer bereft of an identity, the individual was now assured an identity by the collective. He was defined by the collective. The continual scrutiny and evaluation of the individual by the collective promised individual moral growth. One need not wander aimlessly like a Gypsy through the world. The Party provided one with "the right paths and right destination."[52]

One of the boy's liberators was named Mitka. A hero of the Soviet army, a decorated sharpshooter, Mitka is an individualist in a collectivist society. The boy's relationship with Mitka begins to stimulate him to question the claims of the Soviet collectivist mentality. When some local townspeople kill some of Mitka's military comrades, he exacts revenge by executing those who murdered his friends. In so doing Mitka acts independently of the collective, without authority, thus jeopardizing his position in the army, his place in Soviet society.

Seeking to emulate Mitka, the boy concludes that neither society nor the Party can ultimately determine an individual's actions. Rather, it is each individual who must determine his own actions, who must define his own identity, who must create his own meaning. One's self-image cannot be surrendered to the collective, nor can it be granted by the collective. Each person must create his own self-image. The collective cannot insure individual justice. Each individual must engage in his or her own war against injustice. In *The Painted Bird*, Kosinski writes:[53]

> Man carries in himself his own private war, which he has to wage, win or lose himself — his own justice, which he is alone to administer. Now Mitka the Cuckoo had meted out revenge for the death of his friends, regardless of the opinions of others, risking his position in the regiment, and his title of Hero of the Soviet Union . . . Of what value was the rank of Hero, respected and worshipped by tens of millions of citizens, if he no longer deserved it in his own eyes . . . A man, no matter how popular and admired, lives mainly with himself. . . . All the time I thought of Mitka's teachings; a man should never let himself be mistreated, for he would then lose his self-respect and his life would become meaningless. What would preserve his self-respect and determine his worth was his ability to take revenge on those who wronged him.

Having rejected religious faith, demonic belief and collectivistic thinking as tenable sources upon which to base his vision of life, his perspective on reality, Kosinski is left with only one possible touchstone, with a single taproot — the self.

Hide and Seek:
Searching For The Self

According to Kosinski, human existence entails the perpetual quest of an ephemeral subject for an elusive predicate. The self is like a kaleidoscope, continually reflecting the same specks in radically different patterns. Always in a state of flux and becoming, the montage changes just as it begins to come into focus.[54] Life flows on as a series of contradictory episodes. Courage arises from fear, determination from weakness, knowledge from ignorance, love from loneliness. Somehow out of the chaos and the drama of individual existence, one must attempt to forge a vision of the self. To surrender to others the quest for self, to see oneself only as one is seen by others, is to commit spiritual suicide. To become what others imagine us to be would be tantamount to spiritual self-excommunication. In Kosinski's words, "Hell is the inability to escape from others who prove and prove again to you that you are as they see you. Hell is also the inability to be alone, to see yourself as your self sees you."[55]

For Kosinski as for Kierkegaard, the Socratic admonition "know thyself" may be interpreted as "chose thyself."[56] Choice — freedom of action — is an essential ingredient in establishing a vision of the self, an awareness of the self.

The apparently unrelated themes of deformity, sports, illness, and aging which sprinkle Kosinski's works actually coalesce about the quest for self-awareness. Kosinski notes that "awareness of the self must eventually lead to an awareness of one's deformities — physical and psychological. Each of us is deformed; nobody is 'perfectly average'."[57] "Sickness, social conditions, employment, accidents deform us; age destroys us. All of this on a blind date that might end at any time."[58]

Awareness of deformity is an antidote to being stifled by uniformity. Our awareness of our deformities reveals both our limitations as well as our potentialities; it evokes our individuality while it discloses threats to our selfhood. Similarly, sports provides a means whereby the individual achieves a modicum of self-awareness by testing his limitations and capabilities.[59]

In *Blind Date,* Levanter observes himself aging through his involvement with sports, specifically skiing. Kosinski writes:[60]

> Only when he skied was Levanter able to recognize the subtle changes brought about by age ... his body, which had once reacted automatically, was now frequently unable to respond as expected.

Similarly, in *Passion Play,* Fabian the polo-player, observes himself aging. Both activities – sports and aging – act as catalysts to self-awareness. Both preoccupations can transform ordinary experience into drama.[61] Both endeavors evoke a passion for life as well as sounding an alert regarding its fragility.

Both Levanter and Fabian perceive sports as an activity in which the individual competes with himself, and not with others. Neither is a "team player." Competition with others, absorption of the individual into a team, establishes a roadblock rather than a highway to self-awareness. For example, describing Fabian, Kosinski observes, "The essence of competition for him, lay not in the challenge offered by others but always in the challenge posed by oneself."[62]

In order to formulate a vision of the self one must become both the subject and the object of one's thought.[63] One must view oneself from a vantage point from within the self and from without the self at the same time. In *Passion Play,* Kosinski has the protagonist, Fabian, articulate this view, as follows:[64]

> He seemed to himself an explorer in quest of a
> vantage point from which he could more clearly
> contemplate himself.

For Kosinski, a number of such "vantage points" are available. The first is memory.

A feature of one's unique nature is one's memory. No two individuals have identical memories. According to Kosinski, one's memories of the past are not a duplication of the past; rather, they are random impressions of past experiences. Thus, one is the product not so much of one's past as of one's memories of past moments. As one critic of Kosinski's work put it, for Kosinski, " 'I' is the one who remembers. I remember, therefore I am."[65]

Kosinski's cinematic approach to literature is part of a cinematic approach to the self. The self exists as a montage of flashbacks. Without these flashbacks the snapshot of the self in the present is incomplete, incomprehensible. Memories, flashbacks, provide the glue which holds the collage of the portrait of the self together. As Jonathan Whalen, the protagonist of *The Devil Tree,* puts it:[66]

> Now I explore my memories, trying to discover
> the substructure hidden beneath my past actions,
> searching for the link to connect them all.

Despite this search, the link is never found because the view through the kaleidoscope is constantly in flux. In each present moment, memories of the past change. The self emerges as many selves, as many configurations. Memory offers a promise and a hope, as well as a threat and a danger. Describing Fabian, the protagonist of *Passion Play,* Kosinski writes:[67]

> When he contemplated his past, scanned or traveled its corridors, each emerging from an interval
> of years, even decades, he saw not one fixed and
> continuous being, but multiple selves, skins that.
> he had shed, phases of the body and mind now ex-

hausted, abandoned, though alive in memory. His past, then, was a storehouse of what had chastened, enhanced or maimed him while he was in the process of living it.

For Kosinski, choice may determine some of the selves one might become at a given time. For example, Tarden, the protagonist of *Cockpit*, adopts a variety of disguises. Each disguise provides him with an alternative image of himself. However, by chosing his disguises, Tarden, in effect, choses the images of himself he wishes to manifest at a given situation, at a given moment. Disguise thereby enables the individual to be free to create his own image of himself, rather than to have that image imposed upon him. In addition, disguise provides a tactic for self-protection. Through disguise we control the image of ourself which we wish others to perceive; we determine their perception of us; we are granted a glimpse of ourselves.[68] In an interview regarding *Blind Date*, Kosinski observes, ". . . the creative self has many faces. It insists on revealing its essence indirectly through disguises. To Tarden, the self can exist only through disguise: the greater the need for disguise, the greater the potential for selfhood."[69]

Like disguise, memory offers a collage of "multiple selves" which together comprise the individual self. Similarly, in each of one's relationships with each "other", a new self emerges. The self one is with one person in one relationship varies from the self one is with another person in another relationship. The "other" is a vehicle enabling the individual to catch fleeting glimpses of the self. The "other" provides a mirror in which one sees an image of oneself. Without the "other," one lacks even that image. Encounter with others, relationships with others, is for Kosinski, a necessary "vantage point" for contemplation of one's self. Relationship holds forth the promise of "a victory of self-knowledge over detached experience."[70]

While Kosinski's protagonists are loners who cherish their freedom, they are rarely alone. Though Kosinski rejects the imposition of society's ideas and values upon the individual, he nevertheless affirms the need for an encounter with the "other." The compulsion for absolute independence may be desirable, but it carries a price – self-exile.[71] One becomes a spectator of – rather than a protagonist in – the drama of one's own life. While greater safety and greater freedom may lie in detachment, the possibility of infusing individual moments with all their possible meaning is lost. Chance, the ultimate voyeur in Kosinski's writings, never finds meaning or identity; they are imposed upon him from without. Only by means of encounter with an other, especially an encounter with an individual who has retained his or her own uniqueness, can one achieve a deeper awareness of oneself. Describing Fabian, the protagonist of *Passion Play*, Kosinski writes, "He preferred individuals whose singularity gave him insight into himself."[72] In a similar vein, in his interview with *Psychology Today*, Kosinski notes:[73]

> The only way for me to live was to be as close to other people as life allowed. Not much else stimulated me. I have no other passions, no other joys, no other obsessions. The only moment when I feel truly alive is when, in relationship with other people, I discover how much in common we all share with each other.

One way for the individual "to be as close to other people as life allowed" is through sexual experience. Therefore, for Kosinski, sex provides a vehicle for an intimate encounter with an "other" as well as an opportunity for self-understanding. Sex is an arena where risk is required. The encounter held in this arena may end in victory or in defeat, in self-knowledge or in victimization, in intimacy or in exploitation, in the temporary fusion of two lovers or in the dehumanizing degradation of two participants. Sex represents a continuous adventure, a perpetual challenge, sometimes leading nowhere, but sometimes leading through an "other" to oneself.[74]

For Kosinski, the portrayal of sex as entertainment rather

than as "an authentic force of life which is responsible for life itself," is a distortion of "the most human of instincts."[75] Rather than a shield between people, sex can be that which brings people closer.[76] Sex can serve as a channel to the mystery of another as well as a vehicle to the mystery of the self.[77] For Kosinski, it appears, sex is not like an emergency room where "a quick release from discomfort is all one could hope for."[78] Rather, sex is "like walking in the hills. Each time you reached the top of one hill, you see another just ahead and you think that's the top, and then you see still another one, so you keep climbing, never knowing where the last one will be."[79] Sex can be a dead-end; or it can be a pilgrimage. Sex can provide us with an adventure in awareness; it can provoke an experience by means of which we can transcend experience; it can initiate a journey with another toward oneself. For Kosinski, sex can be a key with which one may unlock the most reliable door to the soul. Through sex, one may discover one's own courage and one's own fear, one's own most private desires and one's own most secret proclivities. Through sex one may reveal one's image to oneself as well as to another.[80]

As has been noted above, Kosinski maintains that the self one becomes while with a particular "other" is a different self with a different "other." Through sex one may gain a glimpse of oneself, but only as the self is at a particular moment with a particular "other." Only the "other" knows who one is at that moment. The individual cannot perceive himself at that moment, but only afterwards, upon reflection. The individual is condemned to know himself as a reflection of himself in his relationship with a particular "other." According to Kosinski, "a man is condemned never to know himself as a lover," i.e., one becomes oneself in lovemaking, but one is condemned to know the self he becomes only through the reflection of the self in the "other."[81] The self one becomes can only be known by the self as a retrospective image, as a reflection in the eyes of an "other."[82]

As one is condemned to know oneself through the eyes of an "other," one is never vouchsafed a complete knowledge of the "other" no matter how close and intimate the relationship.[83] For example, in *Steps, Blind Date* and *Passion Play,* the male protagonist discovers that his female lover, the person with whom he has shared ultimate possible intimacy, is biologically actually a man. This is one of Kosinski's ways of expressing the view that the other is never truly known, no matter how intimate the relationship.

In the Kosinskian search for the self, each encounter is replete with promise, each "blind date" is pregnant with possibility. Each moment carries with it the potentiality of enriching and of intensifying life. Each instant offers a new glimpse into a self perpetually in motion. Each moment left dormant is an occasion for regret, a moment to be mourned.[84]

Threats To Selfhood

Two major obstacles impede the quest for the self: the collectivistic vision which society attempts to impose upon the individual and the vagaries imposed upon individual and human history by the omnipresence of chance.

The relationship between the individual and the collective, between the self and society preoccupied Kosinski the social scientist long before it engrossed Kosinski the novelist. Already in one of his masters theses, published in Poland in 1954, Kosinski wrote of the need for the individual to establish self-dignity despite the attempts of society to usurp it.[85] Kosinski's image of "the painted bird" which depicts the struggle of the individual against society, which represents the individual who insists upon asserting his individuality in the face of the hostility of the collective, is not introduced by Kosinski in his novel by that name but in his earlier sociopolitical analysis of collective behavior in the Soviet Union, *No Third Path*.[86]

A group of children caught a sparrow in a trap. They painted it purple, assuming that the other sparrows would "make him their king." The sparrow was set free and flew upward toward its fellow sparrows. The fellow sparrows saw the colored bird and thinking it an intruder and an enemy rather than one of its own, they pecked it to death. This dislike of the unlike condemned the colored bird to death.

The image of "the painted bird" pervades the novel by that name, as well as Kosinski's previous and subsequent works.[87] In one episode in *The Painted Bird*, the nameless boy protagonist is living with a bird trapper named Lekh. The trapper would paint an entrapped bird with a variety of colors and then would let it fly free as a flock of its own species passed overhead. The painted bird would be "vainly trying to convince its kin that it was one of them." However, the other birds would execute their own, thinking it a dangerous intruder.[88]

The Painted Bird is the story of a dark eyed, dark skinned young boy – a Jew or a Gypsy – wandering about rural Poland or eastern Russia during the Second World War. The inhabitants of that region were fair-skinned and light-eyed, superstitious peasants. Like the painted bird, the boy sought protection, solidarity and survival among those who saw him as an unwelcome and as a dangerous intruder. The peasants were conditioned by superstition to consider a person of dark complexion – especially a Jew or a Gypsy – to be an ambassador of the demonic, and were severely enjoined by their Nazi conquerers against harboring such individuals. Living defenselessly in such an atmosphere, the nameless boy was constantly in mortal danger.[89]

In a personal letter by Kosinski, which was published without his permission as part of a 1965 edition of *The Painted Bird*, Kosinski writes:[90]

> Involvement in collective society became more and more forced. Coercive measures trimmed away the vestigial edges of personal freedom. Relentless supervision curtailed away every individual action. This placed a double burden on the youth. During the war years his powers of self-dependence had increased enormously, and the maintenance of personal freedom had been the goal to which he had given all his intelligence and energy.
>
> Previously, while living in the forest villages, the boy had been set apart from others by his physical dissimilarity; now, as a young man in collective society, he was set apart by differences of his way of thinking. The experiences of the war years

made him unable to conform to the patterns of thought and behavior demanded by collective society. Again he was the outsider, the Painted Bird . . .

In his two socio-political studies, published before *The Painted Bird* and written under the pen name of Joseph Novak, Kosinski describes and analyzes the collectivist mentality of Russian life of the 1950's. As was noted above, in one of these works, *No Third Path*, Kosinski compares the fate of the individual who insists upon asserting his individuality to the fate of the painted bird.[91]

As his description of Soviet society unfolds, Kosinski notes that the group — the collective, the Party — serves as the source of one's identity, self-perception, and values.[92] The individual is viewed as a cog in a giant machine, necessary but dispensable should it not function properly.[93]

Each of us is a small wheel in a large machine, and there is no way out of it. You can change places with another wheel, but you can't change the machine itself. You can't live outside the organized *group* . . . The efficient machine [i.e., the collective] which never leaves a man alone, while at the same time pushing him into society, also feeds his mental, spiritual and emotional life.

According to this view of life, "a man is only what others think he is, nothing more. Especially under conditions where the value or uselessness of a man is evaluated by an organized group." In *The Future is Ours, Comrade,* one of Kosinski's interviewees succinctly articulates the position that one's identity is imposed from without and not generated from within:[94]

No one of us may say that he thinks of himself in *his own* terms, because we evaluate ourselves by the eyes of *the others* . . . on them, our fellow citizens, depends our happiness, our creative development, our tranquility . . . Therefore, wherever

31

you go, you are in the collective.
Wherever your collective goes, there you'll go
also!

As a literary artist, Kosinski was necessarily interested in the nature of artistic expression in a society in which one's "creative development" is determined by the collective. In Soviet Russia, Kosinski discovered that art, like everything else, is defined and evaluated by the collective. "Good art" is that which serves the aims of the collective while "decadent art" is that which is considered as harmful to the ends of the collective.[95]

In the collectivist mentality, justice must be defined by those who administer justice for the collective. The ethic of individual retribution, articulated by Mitka in *The Painted Bird*, has no place in the collective. In the words of one of Kosinski's Russian interviewees:[96]

A man is only a man. He must have faith in the
justice of the authority under which he belongs.
If we doubt this, what is left? How will we live
without this faith?

Acccording to this mentality, one should aim at uniformity rather than individuality. "Life has to be waited through." The individual is to be a passive participant in his own existence.[97]

Since his arrival in the United States in 1957, Kosinski has been a keen observer of American life. During the period of his marriage to Mary Weir, he had the opportunity to observe the American political and corporate power structure up close. Despite the American myth of the "rugged individualist," Kosinski's observations led him to the conclusion that the collectivistic mentality seems to be an inescapable feature of social existence. A collectivist mentality – different in content but not in form – characterized the peasants of *The Painted Bird*, the citizens of the communist block, as well as the supposedly individualistic American society. In this regard, Kosinski has observed: "American literature [of the nineteenth and early twentieth century] offered us a vision of a society in which a man was free to define himself. The reality of the society was centered around the concept of the self-made man ... Americans of that period perceived themselves as protagonists in a *drama of life*. They were not yet frozen into a specific social milieu or a single social role ... This is not true any more. Today, even the so-called blue-collar worker has become frozen into middle-class values."[98]

In an interview in *Psychology Today*, Kosinski describes all his novels as being about the victimization of the individual by the institutions of society. This holds true of his works set in the United States, as well as those set elsewhere. Kosinski finds the "popular culture" and "the consumer society" in America to be as indoctrinating, as dehumanizing, and as oppressive as the Russian control of the individual by the Communist Party. [99] The American proclivity toward evaluating the individual by the whims of an often contrived and momentary market, differs in content but not in form from the Soviet method of defining the individual by his present usefulness to the state.

According to Kosinski, the "popular culture" has dwelt upon the oppressors rather than upon the plight of their victims. The reason for this is that individuals tend to identify with oppressors, and find it difficult, if not impossible, to identify with their victims. In opposition to this trend, the focus of Kosinski's work has been the victim. He tries to make us aware of the nature and of the implications of victimization. In an interview in *Contemporary Literature*, Kosinski remarks:[100]

> Popular culture 'immortalized,' of course the murderers – they are best-selling heros – not so their victims. My preoccupation has been with the victims.

In *Steps*, Kosinski reflects the facility of identifying with the oppressor, and the difficulty of identifying with the victim.[101]

Many of us could easily visualize ourselves in the act of killing, but few of us could project ourselves into the act of being killed in any manner. We did our best to understand the murderer: the murderer was a part of our lives; not so the victim.

According to Kosinski, a major source of victimization in the United States is the articulation of the popular culture in the economic sphere, in the "consumer culture." The authentic quest for human meaning and worth is replaced by "packaging," advertising and sales statistics. Reduced to commodities whose value is determined by the fads of the moment, the individual and his quest for meaning become dispensable and easily replaceable by another contrived fad. Hence, for Kosinski, it seems that American culture imposes a definition and an evaluation of individuals which is based upon their current market value. The consumer society advocates the usurpation of the individual's potentiality for assertion of the self. "It [i.e., the popular culture, the consumer society] has taught the man to turn away from himself, to believe that his fate is sealed," writes Kosinski. "The small man who 'made it' into the middle-class assumed that because he had made it, life would take care of itself while he watched it the way he watches TV. He lost the ability to say 'no' to the consumer society, to realize that he shouldn't have bought the house or a big car or a boat, that holds him in debt. In relying on 'Master Charge' attitude to life, he became neither master nor in charge of his existence."[102]

In the Communist countries, Kosinski maintains, the doctrine of dialectical materialism provides a philosophy of history, a script for human events, which seems to offer a source for human meaning while in fact it stifles and suppresses individual freedom and initiative.[103] In the United States, Kosinski observes, individuals often prefer the apparent security of an imposed "plot" for their lives, rather than risk the insecurity of freedom, and the unpredictable implications of individual initiative. Locked into what they hope will be a predictable career, many thereby surrender the creation of their own selves to others.

In his interview with *Psychology Today,* Kosinski notes:[104]

Some of these businessmen are undoubtedly victims of a popular culture that for years has insisted that one's career is one's only "given" plot, a sure way to counter and even to avoid unpredictability in life, the dangers of old age, and so forth.

In dismissing the possibility of many choices which these businessmen could and should make from day to day, by playing up fears and insecurities of growing old, the popular culture has helped to dehumanize their predicament even faster.

According to Kosinski, the failure of the individual to take risks imprisons that individual in the suffocating dungeon of the status quo. The rich, he observes, often fail to take risks because they are afraid of losing what they have.[105] Furthermore, Kosinski notes, professionals readily willing to take risks in their professions are retiscent to take similar risks in their private lives.[106] In other words, many are afraid to risk what they have to become what they may be. Others are unwilling to risk what they are in order to become what they might be.

As society becomes increasingly bureaucratized, as life becomes progressively routine, patterns of daily existence develop which preclude passion, and which preclude instinct.[107] For Kosinski, such a situation is a danger not only to art but to life itself. Without a keenly developed instinct for survival not only human souls but also human bodies become candidates for victimization and extinction. In *Cockpit,* Kosinski tells of a man who had trained a dog to be obedient to his commands. The instinct for self-preservation having been strained out of the dog's nature, the dog's natural proclivity toward independence having been replaced by absolute dependence upon its master, the man was able to beat his dog to death without the dog even turning on him in self-defense.[108]

In *The Painted Bird,* Kosinski describes human behavior reduced to animal behavior. In *Being There,* he compares the unreflective growth of a human individual to the determined and meaningless growth of a plant. However, in *Passion Play* and in his writings on Soviet life, Kosinski describes the dehumanizing reduction of people into machines by the popular culture. The machine is devoid of volition. It acts only as it has been programmed to act. It cannot create its own essence.

For Kosinski, the *innocent* victim of society is to be empathized with and to be protected against victimization. However, the individual who denies his own individuality, who permits society to pre-empt his own freedom of action, is a "dead soul" deserving of dissappointment and regret rather than pity.[109]

In *Passion Play,* the protagonist, Fabian, describes people he has met as follows:[110]

> They appeared to him, most of them, to have consented to the manufacture of their lives at some common mint, each day struck from the master mold, without change, a duplicate of what had gone before and was yet to come. Only some accident could bring to pass upheaval in the unchallenged round of their lives.
>
> It was not contempt he felt for them, merely regret that they had allowed the die of life to be cast so early and so finally. He preferred individuals whose singularity gave him insight into himself.

Describing employees of a bank (The bank possibly represents for Kosinski the Temple of the popular culture.), he notes:[111]

> . . . people [are] so programmed to be efficient, civil, ready with a practiced smile, that the very juices of life had been leeched from their bodies. Like the cash machines that were posted in the

bank lobbies . . . the men and women who worked in banks were to Fabian as functional as the currency itself . . .

Furthermore, Kosinski observes, while the products of technology have served to help us, they also pose a threat to us. By relying so extensively upon gadgets and machines, human beings fail to develop their instincts, even their instincts for self-survival. Many individuals willing only to experiment with gadgets and machines disenfranchise themselves from experimenting with their own selves, with their own lives.[112]

For Kosinski, if there exists a human essence, it is the ability of the individual to assert his or her individuality, to refuse to be reduced to a machine, to say "no" to "group think," to affirm freedom by struggling against predictability, to take the ultimate risk in realizing one's own individual essence.

In *The Devil Tree,* Kosinski observes:[113]

Of all mammals, only a human being can say "no."
A cow cannot imagine itself apart from the herd.
That's why one cow is like any other. To say "yes"
is to follow the mass, to do what is commonly expected. To say "no" is to deny the crowd, to be set
apart, to reaffirm yourself.

The popular American culture, as Kosinski perceives it, has powers of creation which smack of divine omnipotence, and powers of casting spells and illusions which would embarrass even the most masterful magician. For example, the American mass media has the ability to create something from nothing (*creatio ex nihilo*) and to produce images which are perceived as realities. With the power to create like God, comes the power to destroy like the demonic. Whatever the popular culture finds inimical to current fads or simply unmarketable, it has the power to suppress or to cast into stifled oblivion. In his satirical fable, *Being There,* Kosinski dwells upon these themes.

The major character of *Being There* is a shallow illiterate named "Chance." Apparently the bastard son of an elderly and wealthy man, Chance is raised in the man's mansion, never venturing outside of its precincts. Chance spends all of his time tending its garden and watching television. When the old man dies, Chance is forced to leave the mansion. Having no real name, no identity papers, no education and no family or friends, Chance is a man "who isn't there." A selfless self, Chance is a person who has managed "to be *and* not be to be."

Through a series of chance incidents, Chance ends up in the home of an elderly industrial magnate and his wife. Totally a product of the popular culture he has assimilated from watching television, Chance never initiates any action, and always responds to others as he has seen done on television. Thus, Chance is a reflection of the reflections of images he has seen on a television screen. When Chance himself appears on television, the ultimate voyeur becomes his own object of observation. Watching himself on television, Chance – himself created in the image of what appears on the television screen – becomes an image watching an image of himself.

Through another series of chance incidents, Chance comes to be considered a major authority on economic policy, an advisor to the President and a possible candidate for President of the United States. All this occurs because of his responses during interviews with the press and on television. On such occasions, Chance responds to complex political and economic questions by talking about his garden and by responding as he has seen others respond on the television screen. His simplistic responses to complex questions are transformed into statements of profound insight by a mass media in search of a popular culture hero. Thus, a passive and shallow man, a creation of the popular culture imposed by the mass media – especially television – is re-created and transformed into an authoritative spokesman for American politics and economics by that same popular culture, by that same mass media. By chance and through the power of the media, a new image is created. The man – himself but a reflection of an image – is given a new image, a new appearance, a new identity. But, Chance himself is not his new image. He remains in reality only an image, only a reflection of the images he always has seen on the screen.

Unlike the other major characters which populate Kosinski's novels, Chance is not an active participant in his own existence, but a passive product of popular culture. However, like Kosinski's other major characters, Chance is a victim of a collectivistic society. But, unlike Kosinski's other major characters, Chance accepts his victimization, and fails to assert his selfhood. Rather than endeavor to compose a vision of his own, Chance is only a reflection of an image manufactured by the popular culture.

In a sense, Chance is an American "everyman." Like millions of Americans, Chance is a "videot," an incurable television addict whose vision of reality and of himself is a product of "televization."

Like any addict, the television addict surrenders his sense of self and becomes a prisoner of the source of his addiction. The addiction becomes the center of the addict's existence.

Kosinski reminds us that by the time the average American is graduated from high school, he or she has watched about twenty thousand hours of television, an equivalent of nine years of full-time employment. To believe that television addiction has left the addict uneffected and unscared is an untenable assumption.[114]

In an interview with *Media and Methods* Kosinski recounts an experiment he performed while he was teaching. He invited a group of children into a classroom where two video monitors were installed. Television cameras were also placed in the room. While he sat, telling the children a story, a prearranged intruder rushed into the room and began to assault him. The cameras began to film the incident which then appeared on the television monitors in the room. A third camera, filming the children's reactions, recorded that the majority of the children watched the incident passively on the monitors, rather than watching the drama which took place in front of them. What appeared on the television monitor was more real to them than what was occurring in their presence. The image had become the reality. [115] Furthermore, the television offered a means of passive voyeurism rather than an opportunity for active participation. On television the action always happens to someone else. Television reinforces the attitude of detachment and of non-involvement. Kosinski observes, "Television is everywhere . . . Language requires some inner triggering; television doesn't . . . And, I think, ultimately deadly, because it [television] turns the viewer into a bystander."[116]

Whereas literature "assaults the reader directly, as if to say: It is about you", television portrays events that are always removed, distant, occurring to someone else. While literature evokes the sense of self as a passionate participant in the drama of life, television invokes the passive viewing of events and of experiences occurring to someone else, somewhere else.

Like the peasants in *The Painted Bird* who find photographs thrown out of the "death trains," "we, similarly find in the daily newspapers endless descriptions and photographs of atrocities committed somewhere, by someone, to someone," Kosinski writes. "And, like those peasants, the passive onlookers at the grand spectacle of violence and destruction, we, hiding in the privacy of our comfortable homes, watch television programs. Day after day, evening after evening, the images and sounds of human tragedies occurring *elsewhere* leap onto the screens . . . And meanwhile we look at these spectacles in the calm awareness that all these cruelties are happening *elsewhere,* far away, and being committed by *others* who must have their own reasons for acting thus, while we ourselves, though disturbed and outraged; have nothing to do with any of it."[117]

Like Chance, many are satisfied with identifying illusions with truth, complacently accepting images as realities, passively accepting a script written by others as the text of the novel which is their lives, of deluding themselves into equating an enslaving predictibility with personal security. Unlike Chance, the central figure of *Being There*, Tarden, the protagonist of *Cockpit*, refuses to submit to the collectivistic mentality of popular culture. As Kosinski observes, "William Blake warned us that we must all create our own systems or risk living at the mercy of those of other men. Tarden tries to do this."[118]

In his novel, *The Devil Tree*, Kosinski tells the story of Jonathan Whalen, a young and handsome American heir to a huge fortune who attempts to establish a sense of self despite the script society and his socio-economic status seek to impose upon him. In the course of his journey, Whalen encounters the military draft, the Protestant work ethic, the American corporate structure, and psychoanalysis. As Whalen's odyssey unfolds, Kosinski has the opportunity to articulate a further indictment of American "group think."

According to Kosinski, it seems, individuality is only truly permitted in America when it parallels conformity. The dislike of the unlike pervades the American psyche. Deviation is discouraged. Antisocial behavior is suppressed. "In America," writes Kosinski, "you've got to be straight as a highway."[119]

Kosinski views the widespread faith in psychoanalysis among members of the higher socio-economic strata in American to be an example of "group think." For Kosinski:[120]

... the whole process [of psychoanalysis] is intended to make life easier for others, rather than for him [self]. All therapy, from individual analysis to group encounters, is designed to make disturbed patients conform, rather than allow them to discover and live by their own individual emotional truths ... In psychotherapy there is no anesthesia, no clearly defined period of healing, no assurance that things will mend . . . Madness couldn't be understood or cured, but could at least be made socially acceptable.

For Kosinski, neither meaning, authentic identity, nor stability can be provided by society. Often ruled by a collectivist mentality, be it that of the Polish peasants, the Soviet members of the Party, or the guardians of American popular culture, society emerges as more of an enemy than an ally, more an adversary and a threat than a nurturing helpmeet.[121] How, then, does an individual living in society, coexist with society, without violating one's individuality?

My own private, real self is violently antisocial — like a lunatic chained in a basement, grunting and pounding the floor . . . I don't know what to do about the family lunatic: destroy him, keep him locked in the cellar or set him free?[122]

The power of the collectivistic mentality poses an essential threat to Kosinski's philosophy of self. Throughout his writings, Kosinski endeavors to awaken his readers to their own victimization, to their own surrender of self to popular culture. He attempts to make his readers aware of the dangers which a society which celebrates the negation of the self poses to individuals and to society itself. In Kosinski's perspective, the central question most people now ask themselves is no longer, "Who am I?" but rather "who do you want me to be?" Thus, the self-image many perceive "is nothing but a collective image which, like ubiquitous television, engulfs us."[123]

As was mentioned above, Kosinski perceives the task of the novelist as being the taking of society to task, as being the evocation of his reader into awareness. It would appear, therefore, that Kosinski attempts to awaken his reader to the fact that many individuals have become too overwhelmed by the popular culture even to be aware of their own decision to surrender their own individual initiative. He attempts to spur his reader into action, into refusing to assent to being a "dead soul" and toward taking the ultimate risk — to be oneself.

Chance

For Kosinski, the perpetual battle of the individual against popular culture is crucial *because* popular culture is contrived. The restrictions imposed by society upon the individual must be combatted *because* they are artificial. Though they may provide a sense of security, stability, and meaning, they remain illusions, images imposed upon reality. Kosinski warns us of the price we pay for not recognizing the contrived nature of popular culture. He reminds us that we ought not to forget that by surrendering to the artificial constructs of popular culture, we in effect chose to be its victims. We tacitly agree to becoming victims of social crimes inflicted upon us by political commissars, economic entrepreneurs, and "cultural Kapos." We thereby become voyeurs rather than creators of our own existence. The price we pay for this act of acquiescence to the "culture of the denial of self" is the loss of self. Like Chance, we manage "to be and not to be."[124] Like Chance we become "a man who isn't there."

Because the impositions of society upon the individual are *synthetic* they ought to be opposed. They are contrived threats to individual freedom, choice and individuality. For Kosinski, however, the *real* foe of individual volition is the inexplicable presence of chance, the undeniable role of accident, in life, in nature and in history.

While combatting the ultimately self-defeating, self-effacing, self-deluding, and necessarily pessimistic attempt of society to impose a false sense of destiny upon the individual psyche, the individual simultaneously must confront the challenge posed by the reality of chance. Thus, the attempt to realize individual freedom occurs against the backdrop of chance and necessity, accident and destiny – the accidental nature of much of reality, and the artificial imposition of categories of necessity upon reality by much of society. The element of chance looms large in Kosinski's life and work. A few of many possible examples may suffice. Writing about his childhood adventures in eastern Europe during the Holocaust, Kosinski notes, "that I had survived was due solely to chance . . ."[125]

As was mentioned above, on his way from Paris to California to stay at the home of his friends, Roman Polanski and his wife, Sharon Tate, Kosinski's luggage was unloaded by mistake in New York. Unable to catch a plane that night from Los Angeles, Kosinski stayed the night in New York expecting to fly to California the following day. However, that very night the Charles Manson gang invaded Polanski's home and murdered five people. Only by chance was Kosinski not there. Once more, only by chance did he survive.[126]

As has been noted above, the major character of *Being There* is called "Chance." While the boy of *The Painted Bird* is the victim of a series of unfortunate random experiences, Chance is the naive beneficiary of a series of fortuitous chance occurrences.

Kosinski's view, influenced by his own experiences, may be summarized in his own words.[127]

. . . To me, the formidable purpose of life is to perceive it as a drama plotted not by design but by chance . . .

According to Kosinski, chance is an ontological category. Chance is an essential feature of nature, a pervasive characteristic of daily existence, and an inescapable component in the artistic process. From this understanding of the centrality of chance in the natural and the social realms, Kosinski develops a vision of individual action, and of personal morality.

Like Levanter, the protagonist of *Blind Date*, Kosinski's position on the role of chance was influenced by the views of the Nobel Prize winning scientist, Jacques Monod. A friend of Kosinski's, Monod appears in Kosinski's novel *Blind Date,* where he is quoted as saying:[128]

... Your friend Romarkin doesn't dare to admit that blind chance and nothing else is responsible for each random event of his life. Instead, he is searching for a religion that, like Marxism, will assure him that man's destiny is spelled out in the central plot of life. Meanwhile, believing in the existence of an orderly, predetermined life scheme, Romarkin by-passes the drama of each unique instance of his own existence. Yet, to accept a notion of destiny, he might as well believe in astrology, or palm reading, or pulp novels, all of which pretend that one's future is already set and needs only to be lived out ...

In his work, *Chance and Necessity,* Monod maintains that the very existence of life may be scientifically demonstrated to have been the result of a series of chance mutations which could not have been predicted, rather than the product of an evolutionary plan. Since no reason or purpose for life can be given, no system of thought or ethics which presupposes a purpose or a plan to existence can be viable. Destiny is not written in advance, but concurrently with each event. Human destiny and human duty are not products of a preordained plan, but are determined by how human beings utilize the possibilities and the potentialities afforded by the omnipresence of chance.

According to Monod, before life began, its chances of occurring were next to nil. The presence of life is an event which happened by chance. As such, it is a unique occurrence. No scientific laws could have predicted it. No plan intrinsically written into nature could have determined it. In an interview, Kosinski sums up Monod's position, as follows:[129]

The scientific discoveries of Monod and of other biologists led him to postulate a fundamental theory that there is no plan in nature, that destiny is written concurrently with each event in life, not prior to it, and to guard against this powerful feeling of destiny should be the source of our new morality.

Like Monod, Kosinski rejects the propriety of science to impose a plot upon existence in general and upon human existence in particular. The attempt of science to generalize all particulars into universal laws reveals its inability and its unwillingness to confront the presence of uniqueness and of individuality. In *Chance and Necessity,* Monod stated that "science can neither say nor do anything about a unique occurrence. It can only consider occurrences that form a class, whose *a priori* probability, however faint, is yet definite."[130] Similarly, in *Passion Play,* Kosinski writes:[131]

He did the same with the hair that had chanced to grow on his chest. When he pulled it out, he wondered whether the growth of a single hair was an occurrence as unique as the onset of a cancer – or of a thought, of emotion? With all its formidable array of impersonal power and technology, science was able to explain only occurrences that formed a whole class, the genesis of whose origins and behavior – universal, uniform – could be determined and predicted in advance. But science could not explain, or explain away, the unique. What if the single hair he had pulled out was just such a one-time occurrence?

According to Kosinski, scientific discourse like social discourse affirms the existence of "scientifically" established "objective" laws which impose a destiny, a plot, a plan upon existence. Kosinski perceives this approach – in science and in society – to be a contrivance, an unproven assumption, and a potential danger to individual volition.

Taking so-called "scientific method" as its model, social theoreticians have attempted to formulate "laws" of history and "laws" of human behavior in which the human being is a slave of a plan imposed upon his existence, devoid of choice or of self-determination. In *Blind Date,* for example, Levanter feels betrayed by Soviet society which preaches that Marxism offers historical laws "which man has no choice but to obey, and that the State and the Communist Party have a moral duty to enforce at any cost to the population."[132]

According to Kosinski, ideologies such as Marxism, embody no viable claims to objective or scientific truth. Rather, such ideologies are fictions, plots, which individuals or groups of individuals wish to impose upon the lives of others. Lenin, Mao, Hitler and Trotsky, Kosinski observes, were such individuals. They were "fiction writers" who attempted to impose their fictions, their vision of human existence, their political ideologies, upon others.[133]

For Kosinski as for Monod, just as science is unjustified in imposing a plot upon the natural sphere, so is society unjustified in seeking to impose a plot upon the social sphere. Neither nature nor society is predicated upon an objectively verifiable plan or purpose which may serve as a viable basis for human action or for human ethics.[134] According to Kosinski, as for Monod, one must formulate a theory of morality which guards against the notion that destiny may be a source of morality. A viable morality must be grounded in "an ethic which bases moral responsibility upon that very freedom of choice an individual exercises in each instance of his life, an instance being dictated entirely by chance, and not by necessity."[135]

Because of his affirmation of the omnipresence of chance in human life, and because he rejects the notion that life ought to follow a well plotted script, it should not be surprising that Kosinski's novels are devoid of plots. According to Kosinski, a plot, whether in life or in art, is inimical to freedom of action and oblivious to the dimension of the haphazard which characterizes so much of life. Discussing his novel, *Blind Date,* Kosinski remarks that art is the product

47

of the memory of impressions. "The philosophical basis for order in this novel" is not a plot but "the chance selectivity and randomness of our memory."[136] For Kosinski, the life of an individual person or of a literary character cannot be the product of a plot, of a designed destiny. According to Kosinski, the attempt to impose artificial order and predictability upon our lives, is an exercise both in futility and self-deception.

In *The Devil Tree*, Kosinski writes:[137]

... I became aware of how dishonest all people are: we know our lives are chaotic, but we insist that everything happens in an orderly way and that it be logically conceived.

Thus, Kosinski's philosophy of life is reflected in his philosophy of art. If life has no plot, literary works which reflect life must also be devoid of a plot. To impose a plot upon a human life or upon a story about human life forces the unpredictable, spontaneous nature of human existence into an artificial straitjacket.

Rather than offer his readers a plot in the Aristotelean sense, complete with a beginning, middle and end, Kosinski prefers to portray a series of disjointed episodes, strung together in an apparently random sequence. In a sense, Kosinski, the photographer, has influenced Kosinski, the novelist. His narratives read like a montage of snapshots complete with intermittent flashbacks representing recollections of impressions gleaned from experience or from the imagination.[138]

For Kosinski, photography is an attempt to express one's impressions of reality in an imaginative and subjective way, and in so doing to develop a style which could not be copied; i.e., a unique individualized style. In effect, Kosinski articulates the photographic enterprise in a literary medium. His novels are cinematic essays, photographic montages, utilizing words rather than film.[139]

According to Kosinski, chance represents both an obstacle

as well as an opportunity in the human quest for meaning. In *Blind Date*, Kosinski observes that "chance might turn from a benefactor to the ultimate terrorist punishing ... [people] for trying to control their own lives, [for] trying to create a life plot."[140] In *Blind Date*, one of Kosinski's peripheral characters describes human civilization as "the result of sheer chance plus ... people who risked their personal energy and means to achieve certain unpredictable ends."[141] In order to find a semblance of meaning, in order to attain a glimpse of the self, in order to prevent oneself from becoming a "dead soul," and in order to enrich humankind, one must choose to act freely and independently, despite the risks, and despite the obstacles. Despite chance, one must "take a chance."

Kosinski maintains that without the always present precarious element of chance, life becomes monotonous; the drama of existence becomes a tragedy, and daily existence dissolves into tedium. In the final analysis, living with chance is more a challenge than a threat. By utilizing the presence of chance as an opportunity, by denying predictability, by living in a constant state of potentiality, by realizing that each moment "carries the essence of our life," one may be granted the gift of continued awareness of the perpetual marvel of being alive.[142]

Knights In Armor:
The Individual
As Moral Protagonist

Kosinski rejects the notion of predictability and affirms the presence of chance in individual and in human history on moral, philosophical and aesthetic grounds. He considers the quest for causality, predictability and stratification to be a human weakness, rather than a strength. The individual who desires self-definition by adopting a role imposed by society, who lives his life as if it were a script written in advance, thereby surrenders the potentiality of becoming a creator, rather than a victim, of events. In living life as a "role model," the individual becomes like Chance — a product of an image. In so doing, one negates oneself in order to act out a role, to be faithful to a script. The individual relinquishes moral responsibility for his deeds by becoming a character in a drama written by another. Such a person is guilty of moral suicide, of what Sartre calls acting in "bad faith." To such a person, one might say, "You're hiding a dead body. Your own."[143]

Bereft of an anchor in religious faith or in society, the individual is like a tree with branches which must grow its own roots. Once grown, these roots must seek out their own sustenance. The "devil tree" seems to be a symbol of the individual's quest for stability and meaning. The "devil tree" grows backwards: "the roots are branches now, and the branches are roots."[144]

Most of the characters in Kosinski's works seem to have no roots. They are vagabonds, wanderers, nomads.[145]

Through their experiences, and by means of their self-reflection upon their experiences, they attempt to discover who they are, and where they are. By so doing, these nomads become adventurers, these wanderers become pilgrims.

In one of his choices for a motto for his novel, *Blind Date,* Kosinski uses a quote from Jacques Monod:

> Who shall decide what is good and what is evil? All traditional systems have placed ethics and values beyond man's reach. Values did not belong to him; he belonged to them. He now knows that they are his and his alone . . .

With traditional religion, the state, and the "popular culture" unable to provide a viable morality for the individual, the individual must become his own source for moral action. Such action can assume no specific moral code which determines action for a given situation before one finds oneself in such a situation. Kosinski affirms "situation ethics" where moral action emerges out of each situation, rather than being determined in advance by a moral code imposed by society.

Kosinski rejects the notion of predictability on philosophical as well as on moral grounds. The *a priori* imposition of a plot, a role, a script, upon individual action, is but a Kantian act of self-delusion. For example, to "explain" one's present situation and to predict one's future conditions based upon dialectical materialism, or upon career expectations, or upon psychoanalytic theories, is to impose artificially construed categories upon real events. To make such an imposition is to offer a false sense of security, to misinterpret the "facts," to stifle moral initiative, to eliminate spontaneity, and to dehumanize the human protagonist in the drama of his own existence.

In effect, Kosinski's ethic is that of Mitka in *The Painted Bird:* to insure human dignity and meaning, each person must become personally responsible for redressing injustices against himself and against others, where possible, and according to the means at one's disposal. Especially in *The*

Painted Bird and *Blind Date,* the major figures – the name-less boy and Tarden – attempt to execute justice against those who would otherwise remain unpunished for their offenses against innocent victims.[146] Thus, despite Kosinski's obsession with the self, his moral philosophy demands involvement with others, especially with victims. Speaking of himself and of the protagonists in his works, Kosinski remarks:[147]

> They are adventurers but also self-appointed reformers of an unjust world: they interfere on behalf of the weak and the fallen and the disfigured. I see this as an important part of the philosophy of the self: you cannot be faithful to your own sense of drama in your life if you disregard the drama in the life of the others – those next to you.

The motto of *Passion Play* is a citation from Cervantes' *Don Quixote.* This text speaks of the "knight errant." For Kosinski, the "knight errant" must pledge fealty to three existential dogmas. First, he must perceive the vagaries of chance as opportunities for self-discovery and for freedom of action, rather than as threats to the apparent securities offered by stifling predictability. Second, he must refuse to live a plagiarized existence where the script of his autobiography is composed by society and is edited into a definitive edition by the "popular culture." Third, he must realize that in order to slay the dragons of "popular culture" which threaten to consume him, and to confront the tides of chance which threaten to inundate him, he must be prepared to take risks. For Kosinski, the quest for self-discovery demands the taking of risks. As a peripheral character in *Blind Date* puts it, "I'm myself – its the ultimate risk."[148]

Notes

1. Kosinski has noted that, *"The Painted Bird* can be considered as fairy tales *experienced* by the child, rather than told to him."* See Clare D. Kinsman, ed., *Contemporary Authors* (Detroit: Gale Research Co., 1976) 17:417. In *The Painted Bird* (New York: Bantam, 1972), p. 86, Kosinski writes: "The faces around me began to take on the features of the animals in the stories recited, like some live illustrations in children's books which I still remembered." On the differences among the various editions of *The Painted Bird,* see David Richter, "The Three Denouements of Jerzy Kosinski's *The Painted Bird,"* *Contemporary Literature* (Summer 1974), 15:370-385.

2. The boy in *The Painted Bird* was mute for three years. However, Kosinski was mute for more than six years, from 1942 to 1948. See Jerome Klinkowitz, "Jerzy Kosinski: An Interview," in J.D. Bellamy, ed. *The New Fiction: Interviews with Innovative American Writers* (Chicago: University of Illinois Press, 1974), p. 144. On muteness in *The Painted Bird,* see pp. 144-146.

In *Notes of the Author on* The Painted Bird (New York: Scientia-Factum, 1967), pp. 16-17, Kosinski indicates that muteness denotes three things: action speaks for itself rather than having words be a substitute for action; muteness heightens one's sense of alienation; the mute is a silent observer of events.

In *Notes of the Author on* The Painted Bird, p. 249, Kosinski writes, "It mattered little if one was mute; people did not understand one anyway." Mutness is a common theme in Holocaust literature: for example, Gregor in Elie Wiesel's *Gates of the Forest,* Adam in Yoram Kaniuk's *Adam Resurrected.*

3. Peter Black, "New Haven Dedicates Holocaust memorial," *Connecticut Jewish Ledger,* November 3, 1977, p. 1.

4. Daniel J. Cahill, "Life at a Gallop," *Washington Post,* September 16, 1979, p. 10.

5. Ami Shinitzky, "Life is a Drama," *Polo* 5:5 (December

1979), p. 21, claims sixty million. According to Kosinski, the correct number is about sixteen million.

6. Unless otherwise noted, the following editions of Kosinski's novels are utilized in the present study: *The Painted Bird* (New York: Bantam, 1972); *Steps* (New York: Bantam, 1969), *Being There* (Bantam, 1972), *The Devil Tree* (New York: Bantam, 1981), *Cockpit* (New York: Bantam, 1976), *Blind Date* (New York: Bantam, 1978), *Passion Play* (New York, Bantam, 1980).

7. Cahill, "Life at a Gallop," p. 10.

8. Ibid.

9. Jerzy Kosinski, "Time to Spare," *New York Times*, May 21, 1979, Section Two, p. 1.

10. Kosinski, *Devil Tree*, p. 5.

11. Christopher Evans, "Jerzy Kosinski: Passionate Player," *The Minneapolis Star—Saturday Magazine*, September 22, 1979, p. 11.

12. The preceding biographical sketch is based upon an interviews with Kosinski in New York in July 1980 and August 1981, and, the following published references: Addendi to Bantam paperback editions (noted above) of Kosinski's work entitled "On Kosinski"; Rocco Landesman, "An Interview with Jerzy Kosinski," in G. Plimpton, ed., *Writers at Work* (New York: Penguin, 1981), pp. 313-339; Klinkowitz, "Jerzy Kosinski: An Interview," pp. 142-169; Geoffrey Movius, "A Conversation with Jerzy Kosinski," *New Boston Review* 1:3 (Winter 1975), pp. 3-6; Gail Sheehy, "The Psychological Novelist as Portable Man," *Psychology Today* 11:7 (December 1977), pp. 52-56, 126-127; Daniel J. Cahill, "An Interview with Jerzy Kosinski on *Blind Date*," *Contemporary Literature* 19:2 (Spring 1978), pp. 133-142; Cahill, "Life at a Gallop," p. 10; Evans "Jerzy Kosinski: Passionate Player," pp. 8-11; Cahill, "Jerzy Kosinski: A Play on Passion," *Chicago Review* 32:1 (Summer 1980), pp. 118-134; Cahill, "Kosinski and his Critics," *The North American Review* (March 1980), pp. 66-68; Cameron Northouse and Donna Northouse, "Van Home of the Mind: An Interview with Jerzy Kosinski," *Lone Star Book Review*, November 1979, pp. 1, 7, 24; Linda Cross, "Kosinski on Skiing," *Skiing* (November 1977), pp. 143-144, 236; Jerome Klinkowitz, *Literary Disruptions: The Making of a Post-Contemporary American Fiction* (Chicago: University of Illinois Press, 1975), pp. 82-102; Shinitzky, "Life is a Drama," pp. 21-23, 44; Kinsman, ed.,

Contemporary Authors, 17:416-417.

13. Kosinski, *Cockpit*, pp. 16-42.

14. Kosinski, *Blind Date*, pp. 187-189.

15. Ibid, pp. 197-209.

16. Ibid, pp. 237-257; Kosinski, *Passion Play*, p. 21.

17. Kosinski has stated that while *Painted Bird* is *not* autobiographical, nevertheless, "every event is true . . . The bricks are real, but the wall is mine." See *Contemporary Authors*, p. 270; also see Landesman, "An Interview with Jerzy Kosinski," p. 320.

18. Kosinski, *Notes of the Author*, p. 10. In *Devil Tree*, 1st edition, 1974, p. 32, Kosinski writes, "I suspect that whenever I articulate my thoughts or translate my impulses into words, I am betraying the real thoughts and impulses which remain hidden. Instead of expressing myself, I produce a neatly ordered document about someone else's state of mind."

19. Klinkowitz, "Jerzy Kosinski: An Interview," p. 161.

20. Kosinski, *Passion Play*, p. 75.

21. Kosinski, *Notes of the Author*, p. 11.

22. Ibid, p. 9.

23. See Klinkowitz, "Jerzy Kosinski: An Interview," pp. 159-161.

24. Movius, "A Conversation with Jerzy Kosinski," p. 6.

25. See Fredrick Copelston, *A History of Philosophy Vol. 7, Part Two* (Garden City, New York: Image Books, 1965), p. 184.

26. Despite possible similarities with the existentialists, Kosinski specifically has rejected the suggestion that he is an existentialist. See, Nowicki, "An Interview with Jerzy Kosinski," p. 10. Along these lines, it may be noted that Kosinski has admitted an influence of Kierkegaard in an interview in New York, July 1980. Though "Being There" may seem to reflect the German term *Dasein* used by existentialists such as Heidegger and Jaspers, there is no evidence of influence, and, Kosinski uses this term in a radically different manner than they do.

27. Carole Cook, *Saturday Review* 5:27 (November 12, 1977).

28. Christopher Ricks, *New York Review of Books* 22:44 (November 27, 1975).

29. See Kosinski's "Afterward," in *Painted Bird*, p. 266.

30. See, for example, *Painted Bird*, p. 99, 104-105, 233. For passing and implicit references to the Holocaust in Kosinski's other works, note *Steps*, pp. 63, 94-95 (on the apathetic bystander); *Blind Date*, pp. 55-56; *Passion Play*, p. 230:
" 'My relatives died in a fire.'
'All of them?' She turned sharply to look at him incredulous.
"Except my parents. It was arson. One of the biggest fires ever.' "

31. In, Lawrence Langer, *The Holocaust and the Literary Imagination* (New Haven: Yale University Press, 1975), p. 175.

32. Ibid.

33. See Sheehey, "The Psychological Novelist as The Portable Man," p. 129.

34. Kosinski, *Painted Bird*, p. 105.

35. Cahill, "Kosinski and his Critics," p. 68.

36. Quoted in Paul R. Lilly, "Jerzy Kosinski: Words in Search of Victims," *Critique* 22:2 (1980) p. 81.

37. Quoted in Movius, "A Conversation with Jerzy Kosinski," p. 3.

38. Nowicki, "An Interview with Jerzy Kosinski," p. 12; Lorrin P. Rosenbaum, "Jerzy Kosinski: The Writer's Focus," *Index on Censorship* 5:1 (Spring 1976), p. 47.

39. Cahill, "Jerzy Kosinski: A Play on Passion," p. 120.

40. Kosinski, *Passion Play*, p. 200-201, 213.

41. Movius, "A Conversation with Jerzy Kosinski," p. 5.

42. See, Klinkowitz, "Jerzy Kosinski: An Interview," p. 159.

43. Kosinski, *Painted Bird*, p. 132.

44. Ibid, p. 130.

45. Ibid, p. 147.

46. Ibid, p. 183, see also p. 21.

47. Ibid, p. 125. Note *Steps*, p. 37: "But death continued to levy its toll, and children went on dying. Some of the peasants blasphemed God, whispering it was He Himself who had dispatched His only son, Jesus, to inevitable crucifixion, in order to redeem

His own sin of creating so cruel a world."

48. Ibid, p. 197. In *Devil Tree*, p. 10, Kosinski remarks, "But I have realized that, however mystical, no church and no sacrament can protect me against the ultimate threat to my vital existence: losing the sense of my own being."

49. Ibid, pp. 7, 18, 158-160. The desire of the victim to identify with his persecutor is a common theme in Holocaust literature. In *Painted Bird*, p. 153, the boy notes, "In my dreams I turned into a tall, handsome man, fair-skinned, blue-eyed, with hair like autumn leaves. I became a German officer." In *Notes from the Warsaw Ghetto* (New York: Schocken, 1974), p. 39, Emmanuel Ringelblum quotes an eight-year-old boy who screamed, "I want to steal, I want to rob, I want to eat, I want to be a German." See, Bruno Bettelheim. *The Informed Heart* (New York: Avon, 1971), pp. 168-172, 226-227. Members of the *Judenrate* often manifested a desire to identify with their Nazi overlords: See Raul Hilberg, *The Destruction of the European Jews* (New York: New Viewpoints, 1973), p. 146.

50. See, for example, Byron L. Sherwin, "The Holocaust Universe of Arnost Lustig," *Midstream* 25:7 (August 1979), pp. 44-45.

51. *Painted Bird*, pp. 198, 201.

52. Ibid, p. 205.

53. Ibid, pp. 217-218, 227.

54. Jerzy Kosinski. *The Art of the Self: Essays à Propos* Steps. (New York: Scientia-Factum, 1968), p. 35. Note, Kosinski, *Passion Play*, p. 205.

55. Ibid, p. 34.

56. Soren Kierkegaard, *Either/Or* (Garden City, New York: Anchor, 1959), vol. 2, p. 263. In an interview with Kosinski in New York in July, 1980, he noted his fondness for Kierkegaard, especially his work "Equilibrium," where this observation appears.

57. Movius, "A Conversation with Jerzy Kosinski," p. 4.

58. Nowicki, "An Interview with Jerzy Kosinski," p. 13.

59. Cross, "Kosinski on Skiing," p. 143. In *Blind Date* there is much discussion of skiing and of polo in *Passion Play*.

60. Kosinski, *Blind Date*, pp. 23-24.

61. Kosinski, *Devil Tree*, p. 61.

62. Kosinski, *Passion Play*, p. 37.

63. Compare Robert D. Cumming, ed., *The Philosophy of Jean-Paul Sartre* (New York: Random House, 1965), pp. 101-110, 178-181, 188-215. See *Steps*, pp. 60, 44, 132.

64. Kosinski, *Passion Play*, p. 142.

65. Elizabeth Stone, "Horatio Algers of the Nightmares," *Psychology Today* 11:7 (December 1977), p. 64.

66. Kosinski, *The Devil Tree*, 1st ed., 1974, p. 24. Compare 2nd ed., 1981, pp. 22-23.

67. Kosinski, *Passion Play*, p. 205.

68. Kosinski, *Cockpit*, p. 143.

69. Movius, "A Conversation with Jerzy Kosinski," p. 5.

70. Kosinski, *Devil Tree*, p. 101.

71. Ibid, pp. 19; *The Devil Tree*, 1st ed. 1974, pp. 86-87.

72. Kosinski, *Passion Play*, p. 142.

73. Gail Sheehy, "The Psychological Novelist as Portable Man," p. 128.

74. Kosinski, *Devil Tree*, p. 71.

75. Kosinski, *Passion Play*, p. 8.

76. Cameron Northouse and Donna Northouse, "Van Home of the Mind," p. 24.

77. Kosinski, *Devil Tree*, p. 160.

78. Ibid, p. 88.

79. Ibid, p. 79.

80. See, Nowicki, "An Interview with Jerzy Kosinski," p. 10.

81. Kosinski, *Steps*, p. 25.

82. Kosinski, *Blind Date*, p. 216.

83. Note the relationship between Levanter and Serena in *Blind Date*, pp. 215-216. Though they have been lovers over an extended period of time, Levanter knows virtually nothing about Serena's private life or about her private self.

84. See, Sheehy, "The Psychological Novelist as Portable

Man," pp. 55-56.

85. Jerome Klinkowitz, *Literary Disruptions*, p. 85. Elsewhere, Kosinski has noted, "I guess I'm preoccupied in my nonfiction and in my novels with—what interests me most—the relationship between the individual and the group." See, Klinkowitz, "Jerzy Kosinski: An Interview," p. 164.

86. Joseph Novak (Jerzy Kosinski). *No Third Path* (New York: Doubleday, 1962), p. 107. Elsewhere (epilogue to *Painted Bird*, p. 257), Kosinski claims that the image of the painted bird is based on the behavior of peasants he witnessed as a child in eastern Europe.

87. See, for example, Kosinski's description of an albino negress in *Passion Play*, p. 183-184.

88. Kosinski, *Painted Bird*, p. 50.

89. *Painted Bird* may be read as a parable of Jewish history. The defenseless boy described in this book wanders from place to place, surviving because of his wits and the vagaries of chance. The history of the Jews wandering from country to country, seeking a strategy for survival in a hostile environment, seems to be represented by this work.

90. Quoted in Klinkowitz, *Literary Disruptions*, pp. 87-88, from the first edition of *The Painted Bird* (Boston: Houghton Mifflin, 1965), p. 271.

91. Kosinski (Novak), *No Third Path*, p. 107.

92. Ibid, p. 28.

93. Kosinski (Novak), *The Future is Ours, Comrade* (Garden City, New York: Doubleday, 1960), pp. 213, 35.

94. Ibid, pp. 35, 27; also see, *Painted Bird*, p. 203: "At every moment he was measured by yardsticks of professional proficiency, family origin, collective as party success, and compared with other men who might replace him at any time or who might be replaced by him."

95. Kosinski (Novak), *No Third Path*, pp. 84, 57.

96. Ibid, p. 137.

97. Ibid, p. 53.

98. Movius, "A Conversation with Jerzy Kosinski," pp. 5, 3.

99. Sheehy, "The Psychological Novelist as Portable Man," p. 128.

100. Cahill, "An Interview with Jerzy Kosinski," p. 137, and, Kosinski, *Painted Bird,* epilogue, pps. 256-257.

101. *Steps,* p. 95, see also p. 146. Also note the discussion of the victimization of Russian Jewry in Kosinski (Novak), *The Future is Ours,* pp. 224-242. Kosinski was among the first in the United States to draw attention to the plight of Russian Jewry.

102. Nowicki, "An Interview with Jerzy Kosinski," p. 13.

103. See, for example Kosinski (Novak), *No Third Path,* p. 352.

104. Sheehy, "The Psychological Novelist as Portable Man," p. 128.

105. Kosinski, *Blind Date,* p. 201.

106. Kosinski, *Cockpit,* p. 151.

107. Kosinski, *The Art of the Self,* p. 27.

108. Kosinski, *Cockpit,* p. 118.

109. See the episode about "Robot" in Kosinski, *Blind Date,* pp. 46-48, and the episode about the "Mountie Hat Girl," in *Passion Play,* pp. 158-174. For the use of the term "dead souls" taken from Gogol, see Kosinski, *Cockpit,* p. 42. Also note, Jerzy Kosinski, "Dead Souls on Campus," *New York Times,* October 13, 1970, p. 45.

110. Kosinski, *Passion Play,* pp. 141-142.

111. Ibid, p. 274.

112. Kosinski, *Cockpit,* p. 165.

113. Kosinski, *Devil Tree* 1st ed., 1974, p. 195. Also, see Kosinski, *Cockpit,* p. 143.

114. Kosinski, *Devil Tree,* p. 45.

115. Jerzy Kosinski, "A Nation of Videots," *Media and Methods* 11:8 (April 1975), p. 26.

116. Landesman, "An Interview with Jerzy Kosinski," p. 355.

117. Kosinski, *Notes of the Author,* p. 20.

118. Movius, "A Conversation with Jerzy Kosinski," p. 4.

119. Kosinski, *Devil Tree,* 1st ed., 1974, p. 122.

120. Ibid, pp. 60-62. See second edition, pp. 69, 73, 75-76.

121. For example, see Kosinski, *Cockpit*, pp. 16-17.

122. Ibid, p. 11. Kosinski's articulation of this problem is reminiscent of John Stuart Mill's discussion of the "tyranny of the majority" in *On Liberty* (Chicago: Henry Regnery Co., 1955), pp. 6-7, 17. One wonders how much influence, if any, J.S. Mill and Thomas Hobbes may have had on Kosinski. Also note, Samuel Coale, "The Quest for the Elusive Self: The Fiction of Jerzy Kosinski," *Critique* 14:3 (1973), pp. 25-37.

123. Kosinski, "Dead Souls on Campus," *New York Times*, October 13, 1970, p. 45.

124. See Cahill, "An Interview with Jerzy Kosinski on *Blind Date*," pp. 135, 137, 139, 140, 142.

125. Kosinski, *Painted Bird*, p. 255.

126. See ibid, "epilogue," p. 273. This episode is reflected in Kosinski, *Blind Date*, pp. 195-236.

127. Gail Sheehy, "The Psychological Novelist as Portable Man," p. 56 and p. 52 where he notes the "overwhelming role of chance in each of life's encounters." See Jacques Monod, *Chance and Necessity* (New York: Alfred A. Knopf, 1971).

128. Kosinski, *Blind Date*, pp. 97-98.

129. Cahill, "An Interview with Jerzy Kosinski on *Blind Date*," p. 135.

130. Monod, *Chance and Necessity*, p. 144. Also note the symposium on Monod's views, published in John Lewis, ed. *Beyond Chance and Necessity* (Atlantic Highlands, New Jersey: Humanities Press, 1974).

131. Kosinski, *Passion Play*, p. 12.

132. Cahill, "An Interview with Jerzy Kosinski on *Blind Date*," p. 135.

133. Klinkowitz, "Jerzy Kosinski: An Interview," pp. 157-158.

134. Monod, *Chance and Necessity*, p. 180 and Cahill, "An Interview with Jerzy Kosinski on *Blind Date*," p. 135.

135. Cahill, ibid.

136. Ibid, p. 139.

137. Kosinski, *Devil Tree,* p. 71.

138. On Kosinski's rejection of the Aristotelean notion of plot, see his *The Art of the Self,* p. 13.

139. For Kosinski on photography, see Movius, "A Conversation with Jerzy Kosinski," p. 5. In *Blind Date,* p. 61, Kosinski notes, "Levanter soon learned that photography by its very nature depended on imitating reality in an imaginative, subjective way ... Levanter began to evolve his own techniques and a style that could not be readily copied." On Kosinski's cinematic literary style, see Samuel Coale, "The Cinematic Self of Jerzy Kosinski," *Modern Fiction* 20 (1974), pp. 359-370.

140. Kosinski, *Blind Date,* p. 251-252.

141. Kosinski, *Blind Date,* p. 99.

142. See Sheehy, "The Psychological Novelist as Portable Man," p. 55, and Cahill, "An Interview with Jerzy Kosinski on *Blind Date,*" p. 135.

143. Kosinski, *Devil Tree,* 1st ed. 1974, p. 38.

144. Kosinski, *Devil Tree,* p. 199.

145. See for example, the protagonists of *Painted Bird, Steps, Devil Tree,* and *Passion Play.*

146. See, for example, *Steps,* pp. 24-36, 37, 120; *Blind Date,* pp. 22-23, 143, 184-185; *Cockpit,* pp. 259-260; *Devil Tree,* pp. 93-95, 152-155. As President of the American Center of P.E.N., Kosinski has been involved with the plight of oppressed, dissident writers, and with the attempt to see justice done on their behalf. Echoes of these efforts appear in *Cockpit,* pp. 172-175, and *Blind Date,* pp. 33-41, 151-152.

147. Quoted in Sheehy, "The Psychological Novelist as Portable Man," p. 55.

148. Kosinski, *Blind Date,* p. 125.

BIBLIOGRAPHY

Primary Sources
(Listed by Date of Publication)

THE WORKS OF JERZY KOSINSKI
I. NOVELS

The Painted Bird. Boston: Houghton Mifflin, 1965 (a heavily censored and corrupted edition, with an epilogue added without the author's permission). 2nd ed.: New York: Pocket Books (paperback), 1966 (a restoration of the author's original text). 3rd ed.: New York: Modern Library, 1970 (newly revised edition). New York: Bantam, 1972 (paperback of 1970 edition; this edition is utilized in the present work).

Steps. New York: Random House, 1968. New York: Bantam (paperback), 1969 (this edition is utilized in the present work).

Being There. New York: Harcourt, Brace, Jovanovich, 1971. New York: Bantam (paperback), 1972 (this edition is utilized in the present work).

The Devil Tree. New York: Harcourt, Brace, Jovanovich, 1973. New York: Bantam (paperback), 1974. 2nd ed.: New York: St. Martin's Press, 1981, and, New York: Bantam (paperback), 1981 (unless otherwise stated, this revised and expanded edition is utilized in the present work).

Cockpit. Boston: Houghton Mifflin, 1975. New York: Bantam (paperback), 1976 (this edition is utilized in the present work).

Blind Date. Boston: Houghton Mifflin, 1977. New York: Bantam (paperback), 1978 (this edition is utilized in the present work).

Passion Play. New York: St. Martin's Press, 1979. 2nd ed.: New York: Bantam (paperback), 1980 (incorporates minor changes not found in the first edition; unless otherwise noted, this revised edition is utilized in the present work).

Pinball. New York: Bantam, 1982.

II. SCHOLARSHIP AND CRITICISM

Documents Concerning the Struggle of Man: Reminiscences of the Members of the Proletariat (published in Polish). Published as a booklet by the Scientific Society of Lodz, Poland, 1955, and, in *The Review of Social and Historical Sciences* (Polish) (1954) 4:411-432.

The Program of the People's Revolution of Jakob Jaworski (published in Polish). Published as a booklet by the Scientific Society of Lodz, Poland, 1955, and, in *The Review of Social and Historical Sciences* (Polish) (1954) 5:207-236.

American Sociology: Selected Works (in Polish, edited by J. Kosinski). New York: Polish Institute of Arts and Letters, 1958.

The Future is Ours, Comrade (under the pseud.: Joseph Novak). Garden City, N.Y.: Doubleday, 1960 (this edition is utilized in the present work). New York: Dutton, 1964.

No Third Path (under the pseud.: Joseph Novak). Garden City, N.Y.: Doubleday, 1962.

Notes of the Author on The Painted Bird. New York: Scientia-Factum, 1965.

The Art of the Self: Essays à propos Steps. New York: Scientia-Factum, 1968.

III. ESSAYS AND ARTICLES (Selected)

"Dead Souls on Campus," *New York Times,* October 13, 1970, p. 20.

"Dead Souls on Campus," *New York Times,* April 25, 1971, p. 59.

"The Reality Behind Words," *New York Times,* October 3, 1971, p. 23.

"The Lone Wolf," *American Scholar* (Fall 1972), 41:513-519.

"To Hold a Pen," *American Scholar* (Fall 1973), 42:555-567.

"Packaged Passion," *American Scholar* (Spring 1973), 42:193-204.

"To Hold a Pen," *American Scholar* (Fall 1973), 42:555-567.

"Packaged Passion," *American Scholar* (Spring 1973), 42:193-204.

"A Nation of Videots," *Media and Methods 11:8* (April 1975), pp. 24-32, 52-53.

" 'The Banned Book' As Psychological Drug – A Parody," *Media and Methods,* January 1977.

"Our 'Predigested, Prepackaged Pop Culture' – A Novelist's View," *U.S. News and World Report* 86:1 (January 8, 1979), pp. 52-53.

"Time to Spare," *New York Times,* May 21, 1979, Section Two, p.1.

"The Quotations of Chauncey Gardiner," n.d., n.p.

IV. INTERVIEWS WITH KOSINSKI

Klinkowitz, Jerome, "Jerzy Kosinski: An Interview," *Fiction International* (Fall 1973), 1:30-48. Reprinted in J.D. Bellamy, ed., *The New Fiction: Interviews with Innovative American Writers.* Chicago, University of Illinois Press, 1974, pp. 142-169.

Movius, Geoffrey, "A Conversation with Jerzy Kosinski," *New Boston Review* 1:3 (Winter 1975), pp. 3-6.

Rosenbaum, Lorrin P., "Jerzy Kosinski: The Writer's Focus," *Index on Censorship* 5:1 (Spring 1976), pp. 47-48.

Grunwald, Lisa, "Jerzy Kosinski: Tapping Into His Vision of Truth," *Vineyard Gazette,* July 29, 1977, Section A, p.1.

Sheehy, Gail, "The Psychological Novelist as Portable Man," *Psychology Today* 11:7 (December 1977), pp. 52-56, 126-129.

Nowicki, R.E., "An Interview with Jerzy Kosinski," *San Francisco Review of Books* 3:1 (March 1978), pp. 10-13.

Cahill, Daniel J., "An Interview with Jerzy Kosinski on *Blind Date*," *Contemporary Literature* 19:2 (Spring 1978), pp. 133-142.

———————————, "Life at a Gallop," *The Washington Post,* September 16, 1979, p. 10.

Evans, Christopher, "Jerzy Kosinski: Passionate Player," *The Minneapolis Star – Saturday Magazine,* September 22, 1979, pp. 8-11.

Northouse, Cameron, and, Northouse, Donna, "Van Home of the Mind: An Interview with Jerzy Kosinski," *Lone Star Book Review*, November 1979, pp. 1, 7, 24.

Landesman, Rocco, "An Interview with Jerzy Kosinski," in G. Plimpton, ed., *Writers at Work*. New York: Penguin Books, 1981, pp. 313-339. Reprinted from *Paris Review* (Summer 1972), 54:183-207.

(Selected)
Secondary Sources
(Listed Alphabetically)

I. ON KOSINSKI AND HIS WORKS

Alridge, Watson, ed. *The Devil in the Fire.* New York: Harpers, 1972.

—————————, "The Fabrication of a Culture Hero," *Saturday Review,* April 24, 1971, pp. 25-27.

Brenner, Marie, "Social Stamina," *New York Magazine,* June 22, 1981, pp. 26-29.

Brown, Earl B., "Kosinski's Modern Proposal: The Problem of Satire in the Mid-Twentieth Century," *Critique* 22:2 (1980), pp. 83-87.

Broyard, Anatole, "Casual Lust, Occasional Journalism," *New York Times Book Review,* November 6, 1977, p. 14.

Cahill, Daniel J., "Jerzy Kosinski: Retreat from Violence," *Twentieth Century Literature* (April 1972), 18:121-132.

—————————, "Kosinski and His Critics," *The North American Review,* March 1980, pp. 66-68.

—————————, "Jerzy Kosinski: A Play on Passion," *Chicago Review* 32:1 (Summer 1980), pp. 118-134.

Coale, Samuel, "The Quest for the Elusive Self: The Fiction of Jerzy Kosinski," *Critique* 14:3 (1973), pp. 25-37.

—————————, "The Cinematic Self of Jerzy Kosinski," *Modern Fiction* (1974), 20:359-370.

Cook, Carole, "Review of *Blind Date,*" *Saturday Review,* November 12, 1977, p. 27.

Cross, Linda, "Kosinski on Skiing," *Skiing,* November 1977, pp. 143-144, 236.

Cunningham, Lawrence S., "The Moral Universe of Jerzy Kosinski," *America,* November 11, 1978, pp. 327-329.

Kamm, Henry, "Poles are Bitter About Novel Published Abroad," *New York Times,* December 12, 1966, p. 2.

Kauffmann, Stanley, "Review of *The Devil Tree,*"*Saturday Review,* February 27, 1973, pp. 42-43.

Kinsman, Clare D., ed. *Contemporary Authors, Revised Edition,* vols. 17-20. Detroit: Gale Research Co., 1976, pp. 416-418. Revised from 1967 edition, pp. 269-270.

Klinkowitz, Jerome. *Literary Disruptions: The Making of a Post-Contemporary American Fiction.* Chicago: University of Illinois Press, 1975, pp. 82-102, 218-221.

—————————————, "Kosinski's *The Painted Bird,*" *Contemporary Literature* 16:1 (Winter 1975), pp. 126-129.

Knight, Anne, "Jerzy Kosinski, Self-Searcher," *Horizon,* November 1977, p. 96.

Langer, Lawrence. *The Holocaust and the Literary Imagination.* New Haven: Yale University Press, 1975.

Lilly, Paul R., "Jerzy Kosinski: Words in Search of Victims," *Critique* 22:2 (1980), pp. 69-82.

Richter, David H., "The Three Denouements of Jerzy Kosinski's *The Painted Bird,*" *Contemporary Literature* (Summer 1974), 15:370-385.

Shinitzky, Ami, "Life is a Drama," *Polo* 5:5 (December 1979), pp. 21-23, 44.

Stone, Elizabeth, "Horatio Algers of the Nightmares," *Psychology Today* 11:7 (December 1977), pp. 59-64.

Walsh, Thomas P., and, Northouse, Cameron. *John Barth, Jerzy Kosinski and Thomas Pynchon: A Reference Guide.* Boston: G. K. Hall, 1978.

II. MISCELLANEOUS SECONDARY SOURCES

Bettelheim, Bruno. *The Informed Heart.* New York: Avon, 1971.

Black, Peter, "New Haven Dedicates Holocaust Memorial," *The Connecticut Jewish Ledger,* November 3, 1977, p. 1.

Copelston, Fredrick. *A History of Philosophy vol 7, Part Two.* Garden City, New York: Image Books, 1965.

Cumming, Robert D., ed. *The Philosophy of Jean-Paul Sartre.* New York: Random House, 1965.

Hilberg, Raul. *The Destruction of the European Jews.* New York: New Viewpoints, 1973.

Kaniuk, Yoram. *Adam Resurrected.* New York: Atheneum, 1971.

Kierkegaard, Soren. *Either/Or.* Garden City, New York: Anchor, 1959.

Lewis, John, ed. *Beyond Chance and Necessity.* Atlantic Highlands, New Jersey: Humanities Press, 1974.

Mill, John Stuart. *On Liberty.* Chicago: Henry Regnery Co., 1955.

Monod, Jacques. trans. A. Wainhouse. *Chance and Necessity.* New York: Knopf, 1971.

Ringelblum, Emmanuel. *Notes from the Warsaw Ghetto.* New York: Schocken, 1974.

Sherwin, Byron, "The Holocaust Universe of Arnost Lustig," *Midstream* 25:7, August 1979 pp. 44-48.

Who's Who in America 1976-1977. Chicago: Marquis' Who's Who, 1976.

Wiesel, Elie. *Gates of the Forest.* New York: Holt, Rinehart and Winston, 1966.

Typography by: Unicorn GraphiCenter
Chicago, Illinois